Foreword

Neal Barnard, M.D.

Eating a healthful diet can be full of flavor and variety. Molly Patrick and Luanne Teoh's new cookbook, Food for the Body and Soul, give us a wealth of recipes so scrumptious, you'll want to feed them to everyone you know.

Our research at the Physicians Committee for Responsible Medicine has shown that by switching to a plant-based diet and eliminating unhealthy saturated fats and cholesterol that come from animal products, you can maintain a healthy weight, and experience the best of health. In fact, our research shows that a vegan diet can reverse type 2 diabetes, tackle cholesterol problems, and conquer long-standing weight challenges. With a diet based in beans, fruit, vegetables, and whole grains, you'll feel better than ever!

Food for the Body and Soul includes recipes for all levels of experience, so novices to expert chefs are welcome—there is something for everyone! If you are new to a vegan diet and looking for recipes to replace cheese or other animal ingredients, Molly and Luanne have got you covered—with meals like "cheesy" mushroom lasagna, veggie pot pie, and creamy mac and "cheese," you won't miss dairy at all!

We recommend trying a plant-based diet for 21 days, 100 percent, so you can feel the difference. With such a diverse collection of recipes in this book, you will definitely have enough variety to explore vegan cooking for three weeks. Give it a try! I hope that you enjoy this cookbook as much as I have. Enjoy and share with family and friends!

And if you need further advice or tips, check out Physicians Committee's free online 21-Day Kickstart at 21daykickstart.org

Neal Barnard M.D
President
Physicians Committee for Responsible Medicine (PCRM)

Our Story

Thank you so much for being here.

When we made the decision to create this second cookbook, we quit our day jobs, packed up our two cats, sold most of our stuff and drove over 1,000 miles from the San Francisco Bay Area to Silver City, New Mexico.

When we created our first cookbook, Bold Vegan Food of South East Asia, we had such fun creating the recipes, styling the photographs and taking the pictures that we knew we had to have more.

New Mexico was the perfect backdrop to create this book. If you've ever watched Breaking Bad, the landscape in that show doesn't lie.

The rich sky and the vast expanse of open space of the high desert; paired with a quiet that is seldom experienced made it the perfect place to create.

Each recipe in this book was created with love.

We hope to inspire you to eat healthier by showing you that skipping the meat and dairy doesn't have to be scary or unfamiliar.

It's all just food, after all.

We truly appreciate your support and hope that you enjoy the book as much as we enjoyed creating it.

Molly & Luanne

First printing, November 2013
ISBN : 978-0-9897094-0-8

Contact:
molly@boldvegan.com / luanne@boldvegan.com

boldvegan.com

THANK YOU

As they say, it takes a village to get something off the ground. And yes, it really does. Your friends and family play an enormous role in your life, especially when you're embarking into unknown territory by throwing caution to the wind and following your passions and desires like we have.

Our heartfelt gratitude and special thanks to the people who helped make this book happen. Without them, this would not have been possible.

Here they are in no particular order:

Pamela and Joseph Patrick (Molly's parents) - For sharing your home and allowing us to take over your kitchen and turn it into a food lab and photo studio. We wouldn't have been able to do this without your support. We also must thank you for being taste testers, photo editors, prop hunters, prop holders, ingredient gofers and food critics during this process with us. It has been a blast to say the least and we thank you with all of our hearts.

Nicholas Teoh (Luanne's brother) - Our incredibly talented book designer who took on this project pro bono while juggling a full-time job, two kids and dealing with a 16 hour time difference for communications across the other side of the globe. Nick, your work is beautiful and you are a pleasure to work with. Thank you for being a huge part of this little project of ours. Let's do it again soon!

Jenny Fosket (Our friend & Editor) - Our awesomely cool, talented writer and friend who accepted the role as editor despite our non-existent budget. We owe you an unlimited amount of beers and babysitting favors. How did we get so lucky to have you edit our book? We still don't know. Thank you so very much.

Christine June (Recipe tester) - Our paths were clearly meant to cross. Christine, thank you for your thorough, honest and always entertaining feedback.

Mary Rose LeBaron (Recipe tester and dear friend) - Thank you for testing our recipes and for all of your support and encouragement.

About The Authors

This is Molly and Luanne's second collaboration in cooking, tasting, writing, styling and taking pictures together. Published in 2012, their first book of food, Bold Vegan - Food of South East Asia, is a collection of street food from the ten countries that make up South East Asia.

Molly Patrick

I love being in my kitchen cooking with plants. I love it almost as much as I love ~~red wine~~ a hot bath.

I've played with a lot of food in my life. Starting when I was just a little person helping my mom in the kitchen to opening vegan restaurants in New Mexico, Arizona, Texas and California.

Fun for me is taking recipes full of cholesterol, animal protein and saturated fat and turning them into wholesome plant versions that don't taste like Birkenstock foot jam (I know. I can't un-imagine that either).

The recipes that I create will make you reconsider why you haven't eaten more plants before now.

Luanne Teoh

I was made in Malaysia, educated in Australia and now live in America. One of my ~~hobbies~~ talents is eating. I can stuff more food in my face than most people my size.

Being part of a vegan cookbook writing team has been amazing, given my lifelong affair with meat.

I now have a new appreciation and respect for food made from plants and I bring the Asian influence to the cookbooks.

The fact that I am familiar with meat is also the reason you won't find any bird food recipes in our cookbooks. Molly tries to sneak them in but it only sometimes works :)

All photography and food styling by Molly & Luanne

Table of Contents

A Little Extra Love On The Side (Salads, Sides & Dips)

I Need Food Now! (Super Fast Snacks)

Etcetera, etcetera, etcetera (Additional Recipes & Miscellaneous)

Ingredients to get familiar with

Organic Food Note

Buying organic food is best because organic food is not sprayed with pesticides, herbicides and other chemicals to yield the higher crops per farm and to keep away critters.
When we consume non-organic food these chemicals enter our body and can produce unhealthy effects. The cleaner the food, the healthier the body.
Buying local is a great way to purchase organic food while supporting small local farms. Viva la small farms!

Braggs Liquid Aminos

Funny name, awesome product!
Braggs contains 16 amino acids and its main ingredients are soybeans and purified water. Braggs is salty in taste similar to soy sauce but it is not fermented. It is also gluten free. Commonly used as a soy sauce/Tamari replacer in salads, dressings, soups, veggies, rice & beans, tofu, stir-fries, casseroles and popcorn.
You can find it in the soy sauce section of your local health food store.
*It's handy to have in a spray bottle to spritz on food and snacks.

Chia Seeds

Little black seeds with a nutty flavor that have been used by Native Americans for centuries to fuel their athleticism.
When these little seeds come into contact with liquid, they form a gel like texture so they are great for substituting eggs in baking. Their nutty flavor and high protein count makes them great as an addition to salads, fresh juices or even sandwiches. You can find chia seeds in the bulk section at your health food store.

Daiya Cheese

Made from cassava and arrowroot, it is an ideal cheese for people with dairy, wheat, soy and / or nut allergies.
People who are trying to stay away from dairy cheese will appreciate the familiar cheesiness of Daiya. Find it in the refrigerated section at your health food store. You can buy it in shreds, slices or in a spreadable version.

Dulse - Flakes or Powdered

Dulse is a red seaweed harvested from the cool waters along the Atlantic and Pacific coast of North America and Europe. Dulse can be eaten raw, dried or roasted. Its natural briny "ocean-like" flavor is great in recipes that call for fish.
You can find it in the bulk herb section or packaged herb section at your local health food store.

Earth Balance Buttery Spread

A non-dairy butter alternative. Spreads like butter, tastes like butter and most importantly, won't add to your cholesterol. Earth Balance is naturally gluten free.
Find Earth Balance buttery spread in the refrigerated section at your local health food store.

Flax Seeds

Tiny golden seeds with a nutty flavor and high in Omega-3 essential fatty acids.
Flax seeds are similar to chia seeds in their versatility.
They can be used to replace eggs in baking, added to smoothies, sprinkled on hot breakfast cereal, or even used to thicken soups.
The flax seed itself is indigestible. You will need to grind the flax seeds before you use them to benefit from all of their goodness.
Look for flax seeds in the refrigerated section at your health food store.

Glass Noodles / Mung Bean Thread / Green Bean Noodles / cellophane noodles

These noodles are made out of mung beans, are thin like angel hair pasta and gluten free.
They are very quick to cook and they are sturdy and hold together unlike other types of gluten free pasta.
You can easily reheat leftover mung noodles by dipping them in hot water.
You can find them at any Asian market (they could be labeled as any of the above names) or in the Asian section of most grocery stores.

9

Grapeseed Oil

A naturally high heat oil with a smoke point of 421 °F (216 °C). It is derived from the seeds of grapes. You can use this oil in replace of canola or vegetable oil.

Grapeseed oil can be found in the oil section at your local health food store.

Vegenaise Vegan Mayo

Vegenaise is a brand of vegan mayo that is used throughout this cookbook.

There are other yummy brands of vegan mayo out there (like Zesty Garlic Aioli by Wildwood) but vegenaise is our go to vegan mayo.

Nutritional Yeast

Commonly found in large yellow flakes or yellow powder in your local health food store's bulk section. It is a great source of vitamin B complex and B12 (when fortified.) Its flavor is commonly described as cheesy or chicken-like. In Australia it is sold as "savoury yeast flakes." In New Zealand, it is known as Brufax. It is naturally gluten free.

You won't find a vegan's kitchen without Nutritional Yeast.

Sprouted Bread

Made from whole grain that are soaked in water and allowed to sprout.

The sprouts are then mashed or ground and baked into bread. This process retains the vitamins and minerals of the grains so it is easier to digest and healthier than processed bread (as long as you don't have a wheat sensitivity).

You can find a variety of sprouted breads in the freezer section of your health food store.

Tapioca Flour / Starch

Tapioca flour is gluten free and made from cassava root. It is starchy and slightly sweet and popular for gluten free baking. You can find Tapioca Flour (or starch; the term is used interchangeably) in the baking section at your local health food store.

Tofu

Also known as bean curd, tofu is made by coagulating soy bean milk. By compressing the curd, the result are white to yellowish blocks of soft, medium, firm or extra firm tofu. Tofu is a very versatile food, commonly used as a vegan protein. Tofu can be found in the refrigerated section at your local health food store. You can also find aseptic packs in the packed section that are used mainly as an egg replacer in baking.
The recipes in this book all call for firm or extra firm tofu found in the refrigerated section.

Tumeric

Bright orange in color and used in powder or fresh root form. It is very fragrant and is used to flavor curries, rice or as a natural coloring agent. Buy fresh when available and peel it like ginger and mince.
Fresh turmeric will be in the produce section when it is available. The powdered variety will be in the spice section at your health food store.

Miso

A Japanese seasoning commonly made by fermenting soybeans, barley or rice with sea salt. The resulting product is a dark brown paste with a salty flavor. Miso has a very high mineral and protein content and is used most commonly as a soup or seasoning.
Miso contains all of the essential amino acids, making it a complete protein. It protects against radiation due to dipicolinic acid, an alkaloid that binds heavy metals and discharges them from the body. Studies have shown that miso reduces risk for breast, prostate, lung and colon cancers.
It is important to buy organic, unpasteurized miso. Organic because, in addition to the general benefits of organic food, non-organic soy products are very likely genetically modified. Unpasteurized because the pasteurization process kills off the beneficial enzymes in the miso.
You can find miso in the refrigerated section at your local health food store. It may be sort of pricey ($9 - $12) but one tub will last for a long time and the benefits are absolutely worth it.

Food for the Body & Soul

Good Morning Sunshine!
(Breakfast)

Fluffy Vanilla Pancakes

DIFFICULTY **2/5** LEVEL

Time: 15-30 minutes
Makes 9-10 pancakes

NF Nut free if using nut free milk
SF Soy free if using soy free Earth Balance buttery spread and soy free milk

Dry Mixture

1 cup whole wheat pastry flour (150g)
2 cups unbleached white flour (280g)
2 teaspoons baking powder (8g)
1 teaspoon baking soda (6g)
1/2 teaspoon salt (3g)
3 tablespoons sugar (50g)

Wet Mixture

3 cups non-dairy milk (710ml)
2 teaspoons vanilla (10ml)
1 tablespoon lemon juice (30ml)
1/4 cup Earth Balance, melted (45g)
1 1/2 tablespoons chia seeds (20g)

directions

- Place all dry ingredients into a large mixing bowl and gently whisk to combine.
- Place all wet ingredients into a smaller bowl and whisk to combine.
- Pour wet ingredients into dry ingredients and mix until just combined, making sure to not over mix (over mixing will lead to hard pancakes).
- Heat a nonstick skillet over medium heat and melt 1 teaspoon of Earth Balance in skillet.
- Place 1/2 cup (105g) of batter into the skillet, lifting the skillet up and making a circular downward motion to slightly spread out the batter to roughly 8 inches.
- Cook for 1 1/2 - 2 minutes on either side. Repeat until batter is finished. You may want to add a bit more Earth Balance to the pan after every 3 pancakes.
- Serve warm with Earth Balance buttery spread, maple syrup and whatever else sounds yummy.

Time: 30 plus minutes    GF **Gluten free**
Serves 4-6 people   NF **Nut free**

SF **Soy free if using soy free Earth Balance buttery spread and omit the soy sauce**

DIFFICULTY **4½/5** LEVEL

Good Morning Sunshine! (Breakfast)

Biscuits & Chunky Mushroom Gravy

stuff you need...

Biscuits

3/4 cup coconut milk (175ml)
1/4 cup water (59ml)
1 tablespoon apple cider vinegar (15ml)
1 cup tapioca flour (130g)
1 cup rice flour (170g)
2 teaspoons baking powder (10g)
1/2 teaspoon baking soda (4g)
1/4 teaspoon salt
1/2 tablespoon dried basil (2g)
1 teaspoon dried dill
3 Tablespoons cold Earth Balance buttery spread (45g)

directions

- Place butter in the freezer for at least 10 minutes.
- Preheat oven to 450°.
- Lightly oil a baking sheet or place a piece of parchment paper over the baking sheet.
- Combine coconut milk, water and apple cider vinegar in a small bowl and set aside.
- In a medium size bowl, add rice flour, tapioca starch, baking powder, baking soda, salt, dried basil and dried dill. Gently stir to combine.
- Add cold buttery spread to flour mixture and use a pastry cutter or two knives to incorporate. Don't overmix, it will lead to hard biscuits.
- Pour in the coconut milk/apple cider mixture and stir until just combined.
- Place 1 heaping tablespoon of batter (45g) at a time on a baking sheet and cook for 10 minutes.
- Makes 12 biscuits

stuff you need...

Gravy

1/4 cup Earth Balance buttery spread (40g)
1/2 yellow onion, diced (135g)
4 large garlic cloves, minced
5 cups mushrooms, sliced (365g)
1/2 teaspoon dried thyme
1/2 teaspoon dried marjoram
1 teaspoon dried basil
1 teaspoon salt
1/4 cup rice flour (40g)
2 cups of water (475ml)
1 Tablespoon soy sauce
5 turns fresh black pepper

directions

- Melt Earth Balance in a large skillet and saute the onions and garlic for 5 minutes.
- Add mushrooms, thyme, marjoram, basil and salt and cook for 4 minutes, stirring occasionally so that mushrooms don't stick to the bottom of the pan.
- In a small mixing bowl add the water and the rice flour and whisk to combine.
- Slowly add water mixture to the mushrooms and stir to combine.
- Add soy sauce and cook on low for 4 minutes, stirring occasionally until gravy thickens.
- Pour warm gravy over warm biscuits.

Time: 30 plus minutes

Serves 4-6

 Gluten free

 Nut free

 Soy free if you omit the tempeh bacon

Smoky Kale Frittata

1 medium red potato, sliced into 1/4 inch rounds
1 1/4 cup water (295ml)
1 cup garbanzo flour (130g)
1 tablespoons tomato paste (20g)
1/4 cup nutritional yeast (15g)
1 tablespoons lemon juice (30ml)
1 teaspoon balsamic vinegar (5ml)
1 teaspoon salt (6g)
1 teaspoon garlic granules (10g)
1 tablespoon olive oil (30ml) plus 2 teaspoons (10ml), divided
1/2 yellow onion, diced (135g)
3 garlic cloves, minced
4 strips tempeh bacon
1 cup kale, thinly sliced (30g)

directions

- Place potato rounds into a pot and cover with water. Bring to a simmer and cook until potatoes are tender, about 7 minutes.
- Place potatoes in the bottom of a lightly greased round baking pan.
- Preheat oven to 350°.
- In a blender, place water, garbanzo flour, tomato paste, nutritional yeast, lemon juice, balsamic vinegar, salt, garlic granules and 1 tablespoon (15ml) of the olive oil and blend until completely smooth, about 2 minutes. Pour mixture into a bowl and set aside.
- In a skillet heat the remaining 2 teaspoons (10ml) of olive oil.
- Add the onions and saute for 3 minutes.
- Add the garlic, tempeh bacon, a sprinkle of salt and cook for 1 additional minute.
- Place the onion / tempeh bacon mixture evenly over the potatoes, followed by the kale.
- Pour the blended mixture over the kale and bake uncovered for 25 - 30 minutes.

Chipotle Spiced Kale Scramble

DIFFICULTY
2/5
LEVEL

Time: 5 - 15 minutes

Serves 3-4
GF Gluten free
NF Nut free

stuff you need...

1 package firm tofu (475g)
1 teaspoon garlic granules (4g)
2 tablespoons nutritional yeast (12g)
1 teaspoon dried basil (2g)
1/4 teaspoon turmeric
1/4 teaspoon white pepper
1 teaspoon chipotle chili powder (4g)
2 tablespoons Braggs amino acids (30ml)
1/4 cup fresh parsley, chopped (10g)
1 tablespoon olive oil (15ml)
6 garlic cloves, minced
1 bunch of curly kale, de-stemmed and torn into bite-sized pieces (220g)
1/4 teaspoon salt (2g)

directions

- Rinse tofu under cold water.
- Set on a plate or cutting board and take a clean kitchen towel and press down so that the cloth absorbs the moisture. Flip tofu over and do the same to the other side.
- Place tofu in a medium-sized mixing bowl and mash with a fork. Mash until there are no big chunks.
- Add the garlic granules, nutritional yeast, dried basil, turmeric, white pepper, chipotle powder, braggs and fresh parsley.
- Stir to combine.
- In a large non-stick pan, heat the oil on medium/low heat.
- Add the garlic and saute for 3 minutes, stirring occasionally, making sure the garlic doesn't burn.
- Add the tofu mixture, turn the heat to medium/high and cook for 5 minutes, stirring occasionally.
- Add the kale. If all of the kale doesn't fit at one time add a couple of handfuls and wait for it to cook down. It will get smaller once it cooks and then you can add the rest of the kale.
- Once all of the kale is in the pan, stir to combine.
- Sprinkle with 1/4 teaspoon of salt, turn the heat down to medium and cover the pan with a lid.
- Cook for 5 minutes.

DIFFICULTY 4/5 LEVEL

Time: 30 plus minutes   **GF** Gluten free
Makes 10 - 13 crepes   **NF** Nut free
                        SF Soy free if using
                        soy free Earth Balance
                        buttery spread

Good Morning Sunshine! (Breakfast)

Buckwheat Crepes with Lime, Maple Syrup and Toasted Coconut

Crepes stuff you need...

1 cup buckwheat flour (175g)
1/2 cup rice flour (85g)
1/2 cup tapioca flour (60g)
2 tablespoons brown sugar (25g)
1/4 teaspoon sea salt (2g)
1/4 cup Earth Balance buttery spread (35g), melted plus more for cooking
2/3 cup water (155ml)
2 cups plain almond milk (475ml)
1 tablespoon vanilla (15ml)

Topping / Filling

Earth Balance buttery spread
Fresh lime juice to taste
Maple syrup to taste
Toasted coconut flakes to taste

 directions

Crepes

- Place all the crepe ingredients into a mixing bowl and stir to combine.
- Transfer mixture to a blender and blend until smooth, about 1 minute on medium. Pour batter back into bowl, cover and place in the refrigerator for 30 minutes.
- Heat 1 teaspoon (6g) of Earth Balance buttery spread in a nonstick pan (at least 8 inches in diameter) over medium heat.
- Pour in 1/4 cup (60g) of batter in the pan.
- You want to get the crepes thin and round. To do this, lift pan off from heat and move in circular motions while tipping the pan down so that the batter spreads into a thin circle about 6 inches in diameter.
- Cook for 40 seconds to 1 minute until the the crepe has holes and the edges are browned. Flip and cook for another 30-40 seconds.
- Add another teaspoon of buttery spread (6g) after every 3 or 4 crepes to keep them moist.
- Stack the crepes on a plate and repeat until the batter is gone.

Toasted Coconut Flakes

- Heat a cast iron skillet on medium/low heat for 2 minutes.
- Add 1/2 cup of coconut (40g) to the pan and cook until brown, 2 1/2 minutes, stirring constantly.

Assemble

- Spread a little Earth Balance in each crepe, sprinkle with toasted coconut and either roll like a burrito or fold into quarters.
- Drizzle the top with lime juice, a little more coconut and maple syrup to taste.

> **cook's notes**
> · A non-stick pan will make your life easier and your crepes better. If you are using a pan that is not non-stick, you may need to add a little more buttery spread.
> · The batter will seem really thin, this is okay. The batter is meant to be thin.

Time: 15 - 30 minutes
Serves 4

GF Gluten free if using gluten free soy sauce

NF Nut free

DIFFICULTY 3½/5 LEVEL

Quinoa Bowl with Roasted Sunflower Seeds, Kale and Avocado

stuff you need...

1 recipe (2 1/4 cups/370g) cooked quinoa (see recipe below)
1/2 bunch kale, thinly chopped (165g)
1 cup tamari roasted sunflower seeds (see recipe below)
1 cup red onion, cut in half and very thinly sliced (60g)
1 avocado, sliced

Dressing

stuff you need...

Juice of 1 lime
2 tablespoons soy sauce (30ml)
1 teaspoon mirin (5ml)
1/2 teaspoon sesame oil (2.5ml)
2 teaspoons sugar (12g)
1/4 teaspoon fresh ginger, peeled and grated (2g)
1/4 cup olive oil (60ml)

directions

• Place dressing ingredients into a small bowl and whisk to combine.

Quinoa

stuff you need...

Makes (2 1/4 cups / 370g)
1 cup dry quinoa (180g)
2 cups water (475g)

directions

• Place water and quinoa in a pan and turn heat to medium-high.
• Set a timer for 18 minutes.
• Once quinoa has reached boiling, turn heat to medium and bring to a simmer.
• Simmer for the remaining 18 minutes. Turn off heat and fluff with a fork.

Salty Roasted Sunflower Seeds

stuff you need...

1 cup sunflower seeds (140g)
1 tablespoon soy sauce (15ml)

directions

• Heat cast iron skillet for 2 minutes on low heat.
• Add sunflower seeds and cook for 5 minutes, stirring occasionally.
• Add tamari, stir and cook for an additional 5 minutes, stirring frequently.

Assemble

In each bowl, layer the ingredients as follows:
1/2 cup cooked quinoa (65g)
1 cup kale (30g)
1/4 cup sunflower seeds (30g)
1/4 cup onions (15g)
1/4 of an avocado, sliced
2 tablespoons of dressing (30ml)

Potato Latkes with Applesauce

Time: 15 - 30 minutes

Makes 7 latkes
GF Gluten free
NF Nut free
SF Soy free

DIFFICULTY
3/5
LEVEL

stuff you need...

4 medium red potatoes, grated (590g)
1 yellow onion, grated (140g)
2 1/2 tablespoons ground flax seeds (20g) mixed with 3 tablespoons (45ml) water
1/4 cup rice flour (40g)
2 teaspoons baking powder (10g)
1 teaspoon sea salt (6g)
15 turns fresh black pepper
4 tablespoons canola oil, divided (60ml)
Applesauce and sour cream for serving (applesauce recipe to the right)

directions

- Heat oven to 250˚.
- Place potatoes, onion, flax/water mixture, rice flour, baking powder, sea salt and black pepper into a large bowl and stir until all of the ingredients are combined.
- Heat 1 tablespoon (15ml) of oil in a large skillet (preferably cast iron).
- When oil is nice and hot, place 1/2 cup (130g) of potato mixture in the pan and flatten with a spatula (should be about 1/2 inch thick).
- Place another 1/2 cup of mixture beside the first and flatten (in other words, cook two pancakes at a time).
- Cook for 3 minutes on either side.
- Place on a baking sheet and put in the oven to stay warm.
- Place another 1 tablespoon (15ml) of oil in the pan and repeat the process.
- Do this until all the batter is gone.

cook's notes

· You can use any variety of high heat oil you prefer.
· Serve with a side of applesauce and vegan sour cream.

Applesauce

Time: 15 - 30 minutes
Makes 1 1/2 cups/350g

GF Gluten free
NF Nut free
SF Soy free

stuff you need...

5 medium apples, peeled and cut into large chunks. Discard core and seeds (470g)
2 tablespoons sugar (35g)
1/2 teaspoon cinnamon

directions

- Place apple chunks in a medium pan and cover with 3 cups of water.
- Place over medium heat and cook for 20 minutes with the lid on.
- Drain water from apples and place apples in a food processor.
- Add sugar and cinnamon and process until you have a desired consistency. Process for longer if you want smooth applesauce and for a shorter amount of time if you like chunky applesauce.

cook's notes

· You can use a potato masher if you don't have a food processor.
· You can save the cooking water to drink or add to smoothies. It is really yummy.

Time: 30 plus minutes (including additional required recipes)

Additional recipes required
Cashew cheese, page 184
Salsa, page 144
Spiced roasted potatoes, page 200

Makes 4 tacos

GF Gluten free if using gluten free corn tortillas

SF Soy free

DIFFICULTY 3½/5 LEVEL

Breakfast Tacos

stuff you need...

4 corn tortillas
1/2 cup cashew cheese, page 184 (90g)
1 cup spiced roasted potatoes, page 200 (130g)
1/2 cup fresh spinach, chopped (18g)
1/2 cup salsa, page 144 (105g)
1 avocado, divided into quarters

directions

- Warm the corn tortillas in a cast iron skillet.
- Spread 1/4 of the cheese on each of the tortillas, followed by the potatoes, spinach, salsa and avocado.
- Serve immediately.

cook's notes

· If you make the salsa, potatoes and cashew cheese in advance, you can throw these together super fast.
· If you are short on time, you can use store bought salsa.

DIFFICULTY

4/5

LEVEL

Time: 30 plus minutes
Additional recipe required:
pie crust (page 196)

Serves 4 - 6

GF Gluten free if using gluten free
pie crust recipe

SF Soy free if using soy free Earth
Balance buttery spread

Savory Mushroom, Shallot and Leafy Green Quiche

stuff you need...

1 pie crust, either traditional or gluten free (page 196)
1 tablespoon olive oil
1 tablespoon Earth Balance buttery spread (15g)
3 shallots, thinly sliced (1/2 cup / 60g)
4 cloves garlic, minced
1 heaping teaspoon peeled and grated ginger (8g)
3 cups mushrooms, sliced (190g)
5 cups leafy greens, finely chopped (185g)
1/12 teaspoons salt, divided (9g)
10 turns fresh black pepper
1 1/2 cups cashews (195g), soaked in 4 cups of water for at least 1 hour
1/4 cup water (60ml)
1/4 cup nutritional yeast (20g)
1/2 teaspoon turmeric
1/2 teaspoon tarragon
1 teaspoon garlic powder
1/4 cup rice flour (40g)

cook's notes

· You can soak the cashews up to 24 hours.
· Feel free to use any variety of mushroom or combination of different kinds.
· You can use any assortment of leafy greens you like; chard, kale, collards, dandelion greens, etc...

directions

- Make the pie crust and place in fridge to chill (page 196).
- Preheat oven to 325°.
- Heat the olive oil and Earth Balance in a large, deep skillet and saute the shallots, garlic and ginger for 2 minutes on medium - low heat, stirring occasionally.
- Add mushrooms and cook for an additional 2 minutes.
- Add greens and cook for 1 additional minute.
- Sprinkle 1/2 teaspoon of the salt and the black pepper over the mushroom mixture and turn off heat.
- Drain and rinse the cashews and place them in a food processor along with the water, nutritional yeast, turmeric, tarragon, garlic powder and the remaining 1 teaspoon of salt.
- Process the cashew mixture for 4 minutes until creamy and smooth. In a large mixing bowl, add the mushroom / greens mixture, the cashew mixture and the rice flour.
- Stir until everything is well combined. Take the dough out of the fridge and place on a floured work surface. Roll out with a rolling pin until you have a 10 inch circle.
- Place into a lightly greased glass pie pan and pinch around the edge of the crust so the edge is all crimped.
- Bake pie crust for 10 minutes.
- After 10 minutes, place the quiche filling in the pie pan and bake for an additional 40 minutes.

Food for the Body & Soul

Bowls of Goodness and Yum
(Soups and Stews)

Traditional Miso Seaweed Soup with Green Onions and Tofu

DIFFICULTY
LEVEL
1½/5

Time: 5 - 15 minutes
Serves 4

GF Gluten free
NF Nut free

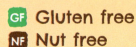

stuff you need...

4 cups water (1.5 liters)
2 1/2 tablespoons dark miso (65g)
3 tablespoons dried wakame seaweed (10g)
3 green onions, thinly chopped – use entire onion except bottom end (30g)
1 cup firm tofu cut into 1/2 inch squares (140g)

directions

- In a saucepan, bring the water to a boil. Turn off heat and add miso.
- Whisk to combine until miso is dissolved. Add seaweed, green onions and tofu and stir gently.
- Cover pan and let sit for 7 minutes.

cook's notes

· Never boil miso. Boiling will kill the beneficial bacteria and your digestive system won't reap its positive benefits.
· Add 1 teaspoon (15ml) of Sesame oil to give it an extra yummy flavor.

Time: 30 plus minutes
Serves 6

GF Gluten free
NF Nut free
SF Soy free if using soy free
Earth Balance buttery
spread

French Onion Soup

Soup

3 tablespoons Earth Balance buttery spread (45g)
1 tablespoon olive oil (15 ml)
4 large onions (9 cups / 860g), cut lengthwise, cut off ends and then sliced into half moons, 1/4 - 1/2 inch thick.
pinch of sea salt
1/4 cup rice flour (35g)
1/2 cup dry white cooking wine such as Chardonnay (120 ml)
1 quart of vegan beef broth (1 liter)
1 quart water (1 liter)
1/2 teaspoon thyme
1 bay leaf
1 1/2 cups (132g) cooked gluten free pasta. Garden Pagodas quinoa pasta by Ancient Harvest is my fave .
1 1/2 cups Daiya cheese, Mozzarella style (30g)

directions

stuff you need...

cook's notes

· Remove bay leaf before serving. Or just make sure you don't serve it.
· If you want a more traditional variation, place croutons (gluten free or regular) on top of the soup (in replace of the pasta), cover with cheese and continue with the regular directions.

- Heat olive oil and Earth Balance in a large pot on low.
- Place onions in the pot and stir them so they are covered with the oil/Earth Balance.
- Add a pinch of salt and stir.
- Cook for 40 minutes on low, stirring occasionally, allowing the onions to caramelize.
- After 40 minutes the onions should be a nice brownish
- color.
- Add the flour, stir and cook for 1 minute.
  Slowly pour in wine, stock, water, bay leaf and thyme and
- stir.
- Simmer for 25 minutes with a partially covered lid.
  Turn off heat and season with salt and fresh black pepper
- to taste.
  Cook the noodles according to the package, rinse with
- cold water, drain and set aside
- Preheat oven to 325°.
  Place oven proof bowls on an oven tray lined with foil or
- parchment paper.
- Add enough pasta in each bowl to fill 1/4 of the way,
- Cover with soup to fill the bowl about 1/2 inch from the rim.
  Sprinkle cheese on top to your taste and bake for 10
- minutes. Turn the heat up to 500° and cook for an additional 5 minutes.
  Serve right away.

DIFFICULTY
1/5
LEVEL

Time: 15 - 30 minutes
Serves 4-6

GF Gluten free
NF Nut free

Bowls of Goodness and Yum (Soups and Stews)

Quick Clear Veggie Soup with Ginger and Lime

stuff you need...

6 cups vegan chicken broth or veggie broth (1.5 liters)

1 thumb-size piece of ginger, peeled and cut in quarters (15g)

2 cups firm tofu, cut into 1 inch x 2 inch rectangular pieces, 1/4 of inch thick - think the size of a Domino (350g)

3 cups cabbage, cut into 1-2 inch bite-size chunks (210g)

1 tomato, cut into quarters

3 green onions, thinly sliced - use all but the bottom end (20g)

1 tablespoon lime juice (15ml)

directions

- Bring broth to a boil, add ginger, tofu, cabbage, tomato, green onion and lime juice.
- Simmer for 30 minutes.
- Serve.

cook's notes

· If you have access to mung bean glass noodles, you can boil them in a separate pan and add them to each persons bowl when serving. They add a nice texture to this soup.

· Do not serve the ginger pieces.

· The longer you let the soup sit the more flavorful it becomes.

Chipotle Spiced Veggie and Pinto Bean Soup

DIFFICULTY
2/5
LEVEL

Time: 15 - 30 minutes (If cooking your own beans)
Serves 6-8

GF Gluten free if using gluten free soy sauce
NF Nut free
SF Soy free if using sea salt to replace the soy sauce

stuff you need...

2 tablespoons olive oil (30ml)
1 yellow onion, diced (210g)
5 garlic cloves, peeled and minced
2 carrots, chopped into 1/2 inch pieces (185g)
3 celery stalks, chopped into 1/2 inch pieces (145g)
1 cup sweet potatoes, peeled and cut into 1/2 inch chunks (135g)
8 cups water
2 cups cooked pinto beans, recipe page 206 or canned (450g)
1 teaspoon garlic granules (4g)
1/2 teaspoon chipotle pepper powder (1g)
1 teaspoon cumin (2g)
2 teaspoons salt (6g)
2 tablespoon soy sauce (30ml)
Juice from 1/2 lime

directions

- In a large pot, heat olive oil and saute the onions for 2 minutes.
- Add garlic, carrots, sweet potatoes, celery, garlic granules, chipotle powder, cumin and salt.
- Stir and cook for 1 minute.
- Add 8 cups of water and simmer for 20 minutes.
- Add beans, soy sauce and lime and simmer for an additional 10 minutes.
- Turn off heat, cover pan and let sit for at least one hour before serving.

cook's notes

· If you are making this soy free then dont add the soy sauce and add salt to taste.

Time:15 - 30 minutes
Serves 4

GF Gluten free
NF Nut free
SF Soy free

Bowls of Goodness and Yum (Soups and Stews)

Thai Coconut Curry Soup with Glass Noodles (mung bean)

Soup

stuff you need...

2 tablespoons olive oil (30ml)
1 large onion, chopped (235g)
5 garlic cloves, chopped
1 heaping teaspoon ginger, peeled and diced (12g)
2 stalks celery, chopped (74g)
1 large carrot, cut into bite-sized chunks (1 1/2 cups / 190g)
1 quart vegetable broth (945ml)
2 cups water (475ml)
3/4 cup light coconut milk (175ml)
1 tablespoon curry powder (8g)
1 teaspoon salt (6g)
1 teaspoon brown sugar (6g)
Juice of 1 lime
1/2 cup cilantro, plus more for garnish (10g)
3 cups mushrooms (165g)
1 stalk of lemongrass. Discard outer most layer and use bottom third only. Cut in half.
3 portions of mung bean noodles (171g)

directions

- Heat olive oil in a soup pan on medium heat and add onion, garlic and ginger. Saute for 2 minutes.
- Add celery and carrots and cook for 4 more minutes.
- Add vegetable broth and water and simmer for 15 minutes.
- Turn heat to low and transfer 2 cups of soup (400g) into a blender along with coconut milk, curry powder, salt, brown sugar, lime and 1/4 cup of cilantro.
- Blend for 1 minutes until everything is combined.
- Pour blended mixture back into soup pot and add mushrooms and lemongrass and simmer for 15 minutes.
- While soup is simmering, boil the water for the noodles.
- Drop noodles into boiling water and cook for 3 minutes.
- Strain and run cold water over the noodles to stop them from cooking.

Assemble

- Place about a cup of noodles into each serving bowl.
- Ladle soup over the noodles, enough to cover the noodles completely.
- Garnish with cilantro and fresh lime wedges.
- Take lemongrass out of the soup before serving.

cook's notes

· Make sure that your vegetable broth is gluten and/or soy free if you are following those guidelines.

DIFFICULTY
2/5
LEVEL

Time: 30 plus minutes
Serves 4-6

GF Gluten free
NF Nut free

Ginger miso soup with potatoes and carrots

stuff you need...

2 tablespoons olive oil

1 onion, diced (195g)

1 heaping tablespoon peeled and diced ginger (15g)

2 carrots, cut into quarters lengthwise and then chopped (2 cups / 250g)

3 medium russet potatoes, peeled and cut into 1 inch pieces (3 1/2 cups / 510g)

6 cups water (1 1/2 liters)

2 tablespoons dark miso paste (40g)

1 tablespoon garlic granules (8g)

1 teaspoon balsamic vinegar (5ml)

1/2 teaspoon salt (3g)

1 teaspoon marjoram

directions

- Heat olive oil in a large soup pot and saute the onion and ginger for 4 minutes on medium heat, stirring occasionally as not tot to burn.
- Add potatoes and carrots and stir. Allow to cook for 30 seconds, stirring frequently.
- Add 6 cups of water, stir, cover partially with a lid and simmer for 30 minutes, stirring occasionally so that the veggies don't stick to the bottom of the pan.
- After 35 minutes turn off heat.
- Place 2 cups of soup (475g) in a blender along with the miso, garlic granules, vinegar, salt and marjoram.
- Blend until well combined, about 2 minutes.
- Pour back in the soup pot and stir to incorporate with the rest of the soup.
- Add a few turns of fresh black pepper and salt to taste.

Food for the Body & Soul

Spiced Black Bean Soup

Time: 30 plus minutes (allow 8 hours to soak your beans)
Serves 6-8

GF Gluten Free
NF Nut free
SF Soy Free

DIFFICULTY
1½/5
LEVEL

Bowls of Goodness and Yum (Soups and Stews)

1 1/2 cups black beans, soaked in 6 cups of water for at least 8 hours (285g)
2 tablespoon olive oil (30ml)
4 cloves garlic, minced
1/2 yellow onion, diced (100g)
1 large carrot, diced (215g)
1 celery stalk, chopped (75g)
1/2 red bell pepper, diced (140g)
2 teaspoons salt (12g)
1 tablespoon cumin (4g)
1 tablespoon ground coriander (6g)
1 teaspoon oregano

directions

- Heat olive oil in the pressure cooker and add onion, garlic, celery, bell pepper, carrot, cumin, coriander, oregano and salt. Stir to combine and cook on medium heat for 5 minutes.
- Add beans and stir to combine.
- Add 7 cups of water and stir again to combine the ingredients.
- Place the lid on the pressure cooker and lock it.
- Place the valve on the lid and turn the heat to high.
- Allow the pot to come to pressure.
- Cook for 35 minutes after the pressure cooker starts hissing.
- After 35 minutes, turn off heat and allow to cool on its own, about 10-15 minutes. If you are in a hurry then carefully bring the pot to the sink and run cold water over the lid until the pressure has gone down.

DIFFICULTY
2½
5
LEVEL

Time: 30 plus minutes
Serves 4-6

GF Gluten free
NF Nut free
SF Soy free

Garlicky Leek and Potato Soup

stuff you need...

3 tablespoons olive oil (45ml)

5 garlic cloves, minced

5 small leeks, use bottom 4th and cut into 1/4 inch rings (1 1/2 cups / 85g)

1 yellow onion, diced (1 1/2 cup / 125g)

7 red potatoes, cut into bite-sized pieces (7 cups / 600g)

2 quarts of water (2 liters)

2 teaspoons dried dill

10 turns fresh black pepper

2 teaspoons salt (12g)

1 teaspoon dried thyme

1 teaspoon garlic powder (4g)

1 teaspoon onion powder (4g)

1 tablespoon nutritional yeast (2.5g)

directions

- Heat olive oil in a large pot.
- Add garlic, leek and onions and saute for 6 minutes, stirring occasionally.
- Add potatoes and cook for 1 minute. Stir so that the potatoes don't stick to the bottom of the pan.
- Add water and simmer for 30 minutes.
- Turn off heat and place 4 cups of soup (420g) into the blender along with the dill, black pepper, salt, thyme, garlic powder, onion powder, and nutritional yeast.
- Blend until smooth, about a minute.
- Pour back in soup pot and stir to combine.
- Salt to taste.

cook's notes

· The longer you let this sit the more the flavor will develop and the tastier it will be.
· Use 2 leeks if they are big.

Time: 30 plus minutes
Serves 4-6

GF Gluten free if not using Gardein
Beefless Tips

NF Nut free

SF Soy free if not using Gardein Beefless Tips

3/5 DIFFICULTY LEVEL

Bowls of Goodness and Yum (Soups and Stews)

Beefy Beefless Stew

2 tablespoons olive oil (30ml)
1 large yellow onion, diced (220g)
5 garlic cloves, minced
2 tablespoons tomato paste (35g)
1 tablespoon white wine vinegar (15ml)
1 tablespoon balsamic vinegar (15ml)
1/4 cup rice flour (35g)
1 quart veggie broth (1 liter)
2 large carrots, cut into 1 inch pieces (290g)
3 1/2 cups potatoes, cut into 1 inch chunks (550g)
3 stalks of celery, cut into 1/2 inch pieces (170g)
3 bay leaves
1 teaspoon black pepper (4g)
1 teaspoon thyme (1g)
1/4 cup parsley, chopped (15g)
1 1/2 packs of Gardein Homestyle Beefless Tips (380g)

directions

- In a large soup pot, heat the oil and saute the onions for 5 minutes on medium heat.
- Add the garlic and tomato paste, stir and cook for 2 minutes.
- Pour the vinegars in and briefly stir.
- Add the flour, stir well and cook for 1 minute.
- Add the broth, carrots, potatoes, celery, bay leaves, black pepper and thyme.
- Stir all ingredients together, turn heat to medium/low and cook for 40 minutes.
- Stir frequently so that veggies do not stick to the bottom of the pan.
- After 40 minutes, add the parsley and the frozen Gardein Homestyle Beefless Tips and cook for an additional 2 minutes.

cook's notes

- The Gardein Beef Tips are optional. The meat eater in your life will appreciate them but the stew holds its own without them.

Vietnamese Pho

Time: 30 plus minutes (take into account the 1 hour sitting time of the broth)
Serves 3

DIFFICULTY 2½/5 LEVEL

GF Gluten free if not using Gardein chicken strips
NF Nut free

Broth

stuff you need...

8 cups water (2 liters)
1 large red onion, left whole (200g)
6 cloves garlic, left whole
1 cinnamon stick
3 whole star anise
1 tablespoon white pepper corns, placed in a cloth tea bag (12g)
2 beefless beef bouillon cubes
1 teaspoon salt (6g)
2 teaspoons soy sauce (10ml)
1 inch piece of ginger, peeled and left whole
1 teaspoon cloves
2 teaspoons lime juice (10ml)

Noodles and Garnish

1/2 pack large rice noodles (7oz / 200g)
1/4 cup shelled edamame beans, cooked (35g)
1 bunch fresh basil leaves or mint
1 handful bean sprouts, ends trimmed
1/2 jalapeno, cut into thin slices
12 pieces Gardein vegan Teriyaki chicken strips without the Teriyaki sauce (optional, see cook's notes)

cook's notes

· We actually prefer thin rice noodles, the thick ones are just prettier to photograph.
· You can add vegan chicken strips by Gardein if you want a meaty texture.
If you choose to do this, place the frozen "meat" directly into the broth when heating it and cook for 5-7 minutes or until it is thawed.

directions

Broth

- Place all broth ingredients into a medium-sized pot and bring to a boil.
- Turn heat to low and simmer for 20 minutes.
- Turn off heat and allow broth to set covered for 1 hour (not essential but will make the broth more flavorful)
- After 1 hour, take ingredients out of the broth so that just the liquid remains.

Assemble

- Heat broth.
- Cook noodles in a separate pot according to the directions on the package.
- When noodles are done cooking, strain and divide into each bowl.
- Pour 2 1/2 cups of broth into each bowl.
- Place vegan chicken and edamame on top of the noodles.
- Place basil leaves (or mint), bean sprouts and jalapeno on the side.

Time: 15 - 30 minutes
Serves 2 - 4

GF Gluten free
NF Nut free

Tofu, veggies and pineapple in Coconut Curry Broth

Curry Sauce Ingredients

5 large garlic cloves, peeled and left whole
2 small shallots, peeled and left whole (85g)
1 square inch of ginger, peeled and left whole (15g)
1 inch long piece of fresh turmeric, peeled and left whole (6g)
4 dried red chilies, stem taken off and left whole
1/4 cup curry powder (25g)
1 1/2 teaspoons salt (9g)
1 teaspoon sugar (6g)
3/4 cup water (60ml)

Additional Ingredients

2 tablespoons grapeseed oil (30ml)
2 cups broccoli florets, cut into bite-sized pieces (115g)
3 cups green cabbage, cut into 1 inch square chunks (155g)
1 1/2 cups lite coconut milk
2 cups pineapple, cut into bite-sized pieces (290g)
2 cups firm tofu, cut into bite-sized pieces (320g)
Juice from 1/2 lime

directions

- Make the curry sauce by placing all of its ingredients into a blender and blending until completely smooth, about 2 minutes. Set aside.
- Heat oil in a saucepan.
- When oil is hot, add the curry sauce and cook for 1 minute, stirring occasionally.
- Add the broccoli and cabbage and cook for an additional minute.
- Add the coconut milk, stir and cook for 1 minute.
- Add tofu, pineapple and lime and gently stir.
- Cook covered on low heat for 20 minutes.

cook's notes

· Asian food can get messy! When you add the curry sauce to the oil it will likely splatter. Have the lid nearby so that you can hold it up to protect your face if the splattering gets out of control.

Food for the Body & Soul

I'm Hungry!
(main meals)

Time: 30 plus minutes
Additional recipe required:
    Red sauce (next page)
Serves 4 - 6

DIFFICULTY 5/5 LEVEL

GF Gluten free if using gluten free
    meatballs and gluten free pasta
NF Nut free if using traditional meatball
    recipe
SF Soy free

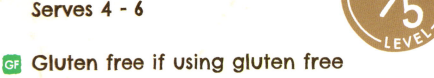

I'm Hungry! (main meals)

Spaghetti and Meatballs

The Pasta

 stuff you need...

1 recipe traditional or gluten free meatballs (see next page)
Red sauce (see right) as much or as little as you want
1 box of spaghetti noodles
Parsley for garnish

directions

- Cook pasta according to the directions on the box.
- Drain pasta and put back in the pan.
- Add red sauce and stir to combine.
- Place pasta in each bowl and top with meatballs.
- Garnish with parsley.

Red Sauce

Time: 15 - 30 minutes

Makes 4 1/2 cups / 1.2kg

 GF Gluten free
NF Nut free
SF Soy free

stuff you need...

3 tablespoons olive oil (45ml)
1 yellow onion, diced (245g)
6 garlic cloves, minced
3 cups mushrooms, sliced (200g)
7 roma tomatoes, diced (450g)
2 tablespoons tomato paste (40g)
1 can tomato sauce (15oz / 426g)
1 bunch fresh basil leaves, chopped (30g)
1/2 tablespoon dried oregano (2g)
1/2 tablespoon dried basil (2g)
1 teaspoon sea salt (6g)
1 tablespoon sugar (15g)

directions

- Heat olive oil in a large pot and saute the onions and garlic for 3 minutes.
- Add the mushrooms and cook for 3 additional minutes.
- Add tomatoes, tomato paste, tomato sauce, fresh basil, dried oregano, dried basil, salt and sugar.
- Simmer on low for 20 minutes.

 cook's notes
· If you make the sauce a day in advance, the flavors will be more pronounced and delicious.

 DIFFICULTY 2/5 LEVEL

turn the page for the meatballs

Traditional Meatballs

Makes 20 meatballs

 Nut free

SF Soy free

 stuff you need...

1 tablespoon olive oil (15ml)
1 cup yellow onion, diced (120g)
4 garlic cloves, minced
1/2 cup tomato paste (120g)
1 cup parsley, chopped (20g)
1/2 tablespoon dried oregano (2g)
1 tablespoon dried basil (4g)
2 teaspoons sea salt (12g)
2 tablespoons water (30ml)
1 1/4 cups vital wheat gluten flour (165g)
6 cups water for boiling the meatballs

 directions

- Heat olive oil in a skillet and saute the onions and garlic for 2 minutes on medium heat.
- In a food processor, place the cooked onions and garlic, tomato paste, parsley, oregano, basil, sea salt, and water.
- Process until smooth, about 2 minutes.
- Place the tomato mixture into a large mixing bowl.
- Add the vital wheat gluten and mix with a wooden spoon until you can't mix it anymore. Then, take your hands and knead it until it comes together in a ball.
- Set aside.
- Preheat the oven to 350°.
- Heat 6 cups of water in a medium-sized pan.
- Take the gluten dough and roll out the meatballs by scooping about 1 tablespoon of dough at a time and rolling it in between the palms of your hands until a round ball is formed. Meatballs should weigh between 22-24g each and measure 1 inch in diameter.
- When the water comes to a boil, place the meatballs into the boiling water and cook until they rise up to the surface of the water, about 5 minutes.
- Using a slotted spoon, take them from the water and place them on a lightly oiled baking sheet.
- Bake for 30 minutes, turning them over after 15 minutes.

 cook's notes
You may need to add the meatballs to the boiling water in two batches as not to overcrowd

continued from spaghetti & meatballs

I'm Hungry! (main meals)

Gluten Free Meatballs

Makes 40-43 meatballs

 Gluten free

 Soy free

 stuff you need...

1 cup dry lentils (180g)
1/2 cup dry millet (95g)
1 small yellow onion, diced (105g)
1/2 cup beet, grated, (50g)
1 cup walnuts, chopped (90g)
1/4 cup tomato paste (60g)
1 cup parsley, chopped (20g)
1 teaspoon dried oregano
1 teaspoon dried basil
1 teaspoon garlic powder (4g)
2 teaspoons salt (12g)
1/2 cup water (125ml)
1/4 cup rice flour (35g)

directions

- Cook lentils by bringing 4 cups of water (945ml) to a boil.
- Add 1 cup (180g) of lentils and simmer for 50 minutes until lentils are cooked, stirring occasionally.
- Place cooked lentils in a large mixing bowl.
- Cook millet by placing 1 cup of water (250ml) and 1/2 cup of millet in a pan.
- Bring to a simmer and cook for 20 minutes, stirring occasionally.
- Place cooked millet in the mixing bowl with the lentils.
- Add the remaining ingredients, except for the rice flour to the mixing bowl (onion, beets, walnuts, tomato paste, parsley, oregano, basil, garlic powder, salt and water).
- Stir mixture so that all of the ingredients are combined.
- Place the mixture in a food processor and process until smooth (you may have to do this in two batches depending on the size of your food processor).
- Once all of the meatball mixture has been processed, place it back in the large bowl and sprinkle in the rice flour.
- Stir until the rice flour is mixed in.
- Preheat oven to 350°.
- Take the mixture, 1 heaping tablespoon at a time and roll it around in the palms of your hand until you have a round ball.
- The meatballs should weigh between 22-24g each and measure 1 inch in diameter.
- Place meatballs on a lightly greased baking sheet
- Bake for 35 minutes.

 cook's notes You may need to add the meatballs to the boiling water in two batches as not to overcrowd

Time: 30 plus minutes (plus time for soaking
your beans if making from scratch)
Additional recipe required:
Pinto beans page 206 (if not using canned)
Makes 12 burgers

GF Gluten free
NF Nut free
SF Soy free

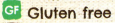

DIFFICULTY 4½/5 LEVEL

Pinto Beet Burger

stuff you need...

1 tablespoon olive oil (15ml)
1 red onion, chopped (165g)
4 cups cooked pinto beans, page 206 or canned (855g)
3 cups raw beet, grated (245g)
2 cups carrots, grated (180g)
1/4 cup parsley, chopped (6g)
2 tablespoons chia seeds (25g)
3/4 cup rice flour (125g)
1 teaspoon garlic powder (4g)
1 teaspoon onion powder (4g)
2 teaspoon salt (12g)
5 turns fresh black pepper

directions

- Preheat oven to 350 degrees.
- Heat olive oil in a skillet and cook the onions for 3 minutes. Turn off heat and set aside.
- In a large bowl add pinto beans, beets, carrots, parsley, chia seeds, rice flour, garlic powder, onion powder, salt, black pepper and cooked onions.
- Mix until thoroughly combined.
- Take a fork and mash the mixture so that the beans aren't whole. You don't have to be too precise in this just do it a few times so that all of the beans aren't whole.
- Lightly oil a baking sheet or cover with a piece of parchment paper.
- Scoop out 1/2 cup (130g) of mixture at a time and form into round patties, about 1/2 inch thick.
- Place on the baking sheet and cook for 15 minutes. Flip and bake for an additional 15 minutes on the other side.

For a gluten free option, use a blanched collard leaf instead of a bun. Here's how to do it (see pictures as well).

Place 2 trays of ice cubes in a large bowl and fill the bowl with water. Set aside.

Use a large deep pan and bring 6 cups of water to a simmer.

Cut off the stem at the base of the collard.

Use a small knife to trim the spine of the collard down the middle of the leaf. Cut it so that the spine is flat with the rest of the collard.

Place collards, one by one in the simmering water for 1 minute. Flip the leaf and simmer for 1 more minute.

With a pair of tongs, place the collard into the ice bath and submerge for 10 seconds to several minutes.

Take out and pat dry with a kitchen towel.

Repeat until the whole bunch has been blanched.

· If your collard leaves are big then it will only take 1 leaf to wrap the burger. If your leaves are smaller then it will take a few. Ideally, look for the bigger leaves. Using 1 leaf will make it easier and less messy.
· You can blanch the collards 1 day in advance if you want to conserve on time.
· Be warned, eating your burger in a collard is more messy than a bun.
· You can top your burger with anything you like, vegan mayo, mustard, ketchup, onions, tomatoes, pickles, etc...

cook's notes

Time: 30 plus minutes (Including citrus jalapeno slaw, beans and green chili sauce recipes. Note that you will have to soak your beans overnight if you are making beans from scratch)

Difficulty Level: 4 over 5 (this takes into account the green chili sauce and bean recipes. Once these are done, throwing this together is not difficult)

Additional recipes required

Pinto or Anasazi beans, page 206 or 202

Green chili sauce, page 198

Jalapeno Lime Slaw, page 188

Serves 4

GF Gluten free if using gluten free corn tortillas

NF Nut free

SF Soy free is using soy free Earth Balance buttery spread

Corn Tortilla and Bean Scramble with Avocado and Lime

stuff you need...

1 tablespoon Earth Balance buttery spread (15g)

6 corn tortillas, cut into 1/4 - 1/2 inch strips and then cut into thirds

3 cups pinto or Anasazi beans, page 206 or 202 (700g)

1 cup green chili sauce, page 198 (260g)

Garnish

avocado

lime juice

jalapeno lime slaw (page 188)

directions

- Heat Earth Balance in a large skillet on medium heat.
- Add the tortilla pieces, stir and cook for 3 minutes.
- Add the beans, stir and cook for 2 minutes.
- Add the green chili sauce, stir to combine all ingredients and cook for an additional 2 minutes.
- Place a portion of the scramble on each plate (or bowl), add as much slaw as you want, and squeeze with lime. Place a half of an avocado on the side of the plate so people can scoop their own.

cook's notes

· If you are pressed for time you can use canned beans. If you are using canned beans then you will need to add 1/2 cup (120ml) of water to the dish when you add the green chili.

Southern Indian Potato Curry

DIFFICULTY
3/5
LEVEL

Time: 30 plus minutes
Serves 4-6

GF Gluten free
NF Nut free
SF Soy free if using soy free Earth
Balance buttery spread

I'm Hungry! (main meals)

stuff you need...

1/4 cup olive oil oil (60ml)

1 tablespoon Earth Balance buttery spread (20g)

1 teaspoon yellow mustard seed (4g)

1/4 teaspoon fenugreek seeds

5 dried red chilis, left whole (5g)

5 garlic cloves, peeled and minced

1 large red onion, cut into chunks (260g)

2 medium tomatoes, diced (375g)

2 tablespoons curry powder (20g)

2 teaspoons coriander powder (4g)

1 teaspoon cumin powder (4g)

1 tablespoon red chili powder (10g)

1 teaspoon salt (6g)

2 teaspoons sugar (12g)

Juice from 1 lime

3 large russet potatoes, cut into a little larger than bite-sized chunks (620g)

1 1/2 cups water

cook's notes

· You can eat it right away if you don't have time for it to sit 1 hour. However, the taste and texture will be more developed if you wait. As with most curries when left overnight, the flavors are even better the next day.

· Take out red chilies before serving.

directions

- In a large pan, heat the oil and Earth Balance over medium/low heat.
- Add mustard seeds and cook until they pop, about 2 minutes.
- Add fenugreek, whole red chilies and garlic.
- Stir and cook for 30 seconds.
- Add onion, stir and cook for 1 minute.
- Add tomatoes, stir and cook for 3 minutes.
- Add curry powder, coriander, cumin powder, red chili powder, salt, sugar and lime juice.
- Stir and cook for 1 minute.
- Add potatoes and 1 1/2 cups water, stir gently to combine, turn to low heat, cover pan and cook for 40 minutes. Stir occasionally and gently so that potatoes don't break apart or stick to bottom pan.
- Turn off heat and let sit for 1 hour before serving.

Time: 30 plus minutes
Serves 6

GF Gluten free
NF Nut free
SF Soy free if using soy free Earth Balance buttery spread

I'm Hungry! (main meals)

Shepherd's Pie

directions

stuff you need...

Mashed potatoes

2 lbs potatoes, peeled - any variety will do - cut into 1-2 inch cubes (930g)

8 cups of water

1/2 cup Earth Balance buttery spread (75g)

1/2 teaspoon salt (3g)

1/4 teaspoon white pepper

1/4 cup water (60ml)

Filling

2 tablespoons Earth Balance buttery spread (30g)

1 tablespoon olive oil (15ml)

1 large yellow onion, diced (225g)

3 celery stalks, chopped (190g)

3 carrots, diced (or one large carrot) (1.5 cups / 215g)

1 cup of vegan beef broth

3 large portobello mushrooms, sliced in 1/2 inch slices and then cut across into 1 inch cubes - see picture (310g)

2 tablespoons tomato paste (40g)

1 teaspoon thyme

1 teaspoon sugar (6g)

1 teaspoon salt (6)

1 dash of freshly grated nutmeg

1 tablespoon (15g) rice flour mixed with 1/2 cup water (120ml)

Mashed Potatoes

- Place 8 cups of water and the cubed potatoes into a large pan and bring to a boil.
- Simmer for 15 minutes and then turn off heat, cover with a lid and set aside.

Filling

- Melt the olive oil and the Earth Balance in a soup pot and add onions, celery and carrots. Stir and cook for 5 minutes on medium/low heat.
- Add broth and simmer for 15 minutes.
- Add mushrooms, tomato paste, thyme, sugar, salt and nutmeg. Simmer for 3 minutes.
- Add rice flour/water mixture and cook for an additional 2 minutes.
- Turn off heat.
- Preheat oven to 375° and start making the mashed potatoes.
- Drain the water from potatoes, reserving 1/4 cup (60ml) of the cooking water.
- Place potatoes back in the pot and mash with a fork or potato masher.
- Add Earth Balance, salt, white pepper and cooking water. Stir potatoes until they are creamy and smooth.

*

Assemble

- Lightly oil an 8-inch round casserole dish or cast iron skillet with a high edge and add the filling, spreading it evenly on the bottom of the pan.
- Gently add the mashed potatoes over the filling, 1/2 cup at a time. Take a rubber spatula and evenly smooth out the potatoes.
- Take a fork and lightly press into the potatoes and drag.
- Do this to the entire top of the casserole.
- This will allow some bits to get more cooked than other bits and provide nice texture.
- Place in the oven and cook for 40 minutes.

Time: 15 - 30 minutes
Serves 4-6

GF Gluten free if you follow the cook's notes at the bottom of the recipe

NF Nut free

SF Soy free if you omit the soy sauce (see cook's notes)

DIFFICULTY 3/5 LEVEL

Mushroom Stroganoff

stuff you need...

8 oz. uncooked ribbon noodles (230g)
1 tablespoon Earth Balance buttery spread (15g)
1 yellow onion, chopped (140g)
3 tablespoons whole wheat flour, divided (20g)
2 cups beefless beef broth or veggie broth (.5 liters)
1 tablespoon soy sauce (15ml)
1 teaspoon lemon juice (5ml)
1 teaspoon tomato paste (6g)
1 1/2 pounds mushrooms (half portobello and half button mushrooms), cut into large 2-inch chunks (740g)
1/2 teaspoon dried thyme
1/2 teaspoon dried sage
1/2 teaspoon salt (3g)
1 tablespoon white wine vinegar (15ml)
1/4 cup vegan sour cream - optional (55g)
10 turns of fresh ground, black pepper
1/4 cup flat-leaf parsley, minced (6g)

cook's notes

· You can make this dish gluten free if you use gluten free pasta, gluten free soy sauce and substitute the whole wheat flour with rice flour.
· If you want a soy free version, swap out the soy sauce with sea salt to taste.

directions

- Cook the noodles per the direction on the package. Under cook them a bit because they will be cooked again once incorporated into the sauce.
- Drain, and set aside.
- In a large saucepan, melt the Earth Balance and saute the onions for three minutes on medium heat.
- Add the flour and cook for 30 seconds, stirring constantly.
- Gradually add the broth, soy sauce, lemon juice and tomato paste, while stirring at the same time. Stir until mixture becomes thick and bubbly, about a minute.
- Add the mushrooms, thyme, sage and salt. Stir to combine.
- Cook for 5 minutes, stirring frequently until mushrooms have shrunk in size.
- Add the vinegar and simmer for 4 more minutes.
- Add the noodles, sour cream, 1 tablespoon of flour, black pepper and parsley and cook on low for an additional 5 minutes.
- Garnish with parsley.

Cheesy Scalloped Potatoes

DIFFICULTY 3½/5 LEVEL

Time: 30 plus minutes (includes cheese sauce recipe)
Additional recipe required: Cheese sauce, page 192

GF Gluten free
NF Nut free

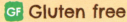

I'm Hungry! (main meals)

Fiery Garlic Tofu

1 14 oz. box (397g) firm tofu tofu, cut into 1 inch squares

6 tablespoons cornstarch (45g)

1/4 cup grapeseed oil plus 3 tablespoons, divided (105ml)

1/2 teaspoon salt, divided (3g)

20 turns fresh black pepper

10 large garlic cloves, minced

3 - 5 red dried chilies, cut in half (more if you like more spice)

1 heaping tablespoon peeled and minced ginger (12g)

1 tablespoon soy sauce (15ml)

6 tablespoons water (90ml)

1 red onion, sliced into rounds (140g)

1/2 teaspoon sesame oil (2.5ml)

Sugar Glaze

1 tablespoon (15g) brown sugar mixed with 1 tablespoon (15ml) water

1 green onion, cut into 2 inch strips for garnish

- Serve with cilantro rice (page 194
- Do not serve the red chilies, they are added for flavor, not to eat directly.
- If you don't like spicy at all then you can leave the red chilies whole.

cook's notes

directions

- Place cornstarch spread out on a plate.
- Cut tofu and dredge evenly in cornstarch. Set aside.
- Heat 1/4 cup (60ml) of the grapeseed oil in a nonstick pan.
- Place 1/2 of the tofu in oil. Add 1/4 teaspoon salt and 10 turns of black pepper.
- Cook for 9-10 minutes, turning so that all sides get brown.
- Take out of pan and place on a brown paper bag (placed on a plate) to soak up oil.
- Place 3 more tablespoons (45ml) of oil in the pan and add the remaining tofu.
- Add another 1/4 teaspoon salt and 10 turns black pepper and cook for 9-10 minutes.
- Take out and place on paper bag.
- Use the same oil and pan and add the garlic, chili and ginger.
- Cook for 1 minute and then add 1 tablespoon soy sauce and 6 tablespoons water.
- Add red onions and sesame oil and cook for 3 minutes.
- Add the tofu back to the pan, stir to combine and cook for 2 minutes.
- Add the glaze and cook for an additional minute.
- Garnish with green onions.

Cheesy Mushroom Lasagna

Time: 30 plus minutes (including red sauce recipe)
Additional recipe required: Red sauce page 186

Serves 8

GF Gluten free if using gluten free lasagna noodles

SF Soy free if using cashew cheese instead of tofu cheese (see cook's note)
Additional recipe required
Red sauce page 186

DIFFICULTY 4/5 LEVEL

Red Sauce (page 186)
Cheese Mixture

1 package firm tofu (14 oz / 440g)
1/4 cup nutritional yeast (20g)
1 teaspoon garlic powder (4g)
1 teaspoon salt (6g)
1 teaspoon dried dill
1 tablespoon lemon juice (15ml)
1/4 cup water

Veggies

1 tablespoon olive oil (15ml)
1 cup onion, diced (115g)
1 cup crookneck squash, or zucchini (105g)
1 cup red bell pepper, diced (135g)
3 cups mushrooms, sliced (235g)
1/2 cup parsley, chopped (10g)
1 tablespoon oregano (4g)
1 teaspoon marjoram (1g)
1 teaspoon garlic powder (4g)
1 teaspoon salt (6g)
2 boxes of no cook lasagna noodles.

stuff you need...

Cheese mixture

- In a food processor, place all of the cheese mixture ingredients and process until smooth.
- Place in a bowl and set aside.

Veggie mixture

- In a large skillet, heat the olive oil over medium heat.
- Add the onions and cook for 3 minutes, stirring occasionally so they don't burn.
- Add the squash, red bell pepper, mushroom, parsley, oregano, marjoram, garlic powder and salt. Stir to combine and cook for 5 minutes.
- Turn off heat and set aside.

directions

✳ Assemble the lasagna

- Once you have all 3 components ready (red sauce, cheese mixture and veggie mixture), preheat oven to 350°F (175°C).
- Lightly oil a 9x13 baking pan.
- Spread 1/2 cup (135g) of the red sauce evenly on the bottom of the pan.
- Add a layer of lasagna noodles (5 noodles).
- Add 1 cup (125g) of cheese sauce over the noodles and spread evenly to cover noodles.
- Add 1 cup (170g) of veggies and spread evenly over cheese sauce, followed by 1 cup of red sauce .
- Add 5 more noodles, 1/2 cup (110g) of cheese sauce ,1 cup of veggies (170g), 1 cup of red sauce (250g).
- Add 5 more noodles, followed by the remaining cheese, veggies and red sauce (in that order).
- Cover with foil and bake for 50 minutes.

· If you want a soy free version, use a double batch the cashew cheese (page 184) in place of the tofu cheese.

cook's notes

Time: 30 plus minutes (take note of the soaking time for the cashews)
Serves 4

GF Gluten free if using gluten free pasta
SF Soy free if using soy free Earth Balance buttery spread

Creamy Alfredo Pasta with mushrooms, kale and onions

1/2 box angel hair pasta (1/2 lb/ 227g)

White Sauce

1 cup cashews (130g) soaked in 3 cups of water (710ml) for at least 1 hour, up to overnight.

1 tablespoon Earth Balance buttery spread (15g)

6 cloves garlic, minced

1 1/2 cups water (375ml)

1 tablespoon coconut milk (15ml)

1 teaspoon lemon juice (5ml)

1 teaspoon salt (6g)

10 turns fresh black pepper

Veggies

1 tablespoon olive oil (15ml)

1 small red onion, cut in half lengthwise and sliced into thin slices (155g)

2 cups mushrooms, sliced (155g)

3 - 5 cups kale, thinly chopped (80g - 115g)

1/2 teaspoon salt

10 turns black pepper

Parsley for garnish

cook's notes

· The longer you soak the cashews the creamier the sauce will be.
· If you want something lighter than pasta, you can substitute couscous, quinoa or millet in place of the pasta.
· If you do use pasta, this recipe is tasty with any variety of pasta you like.

directions

White sauce

- Heat Earth Balance in a small skillet and saute the garlic for 1 minute on medium-low heat.
- Rinse and drain the soaked cashews and place them in a blender, along with the sauteed garlic mixture, water, coconut milk, lemon juice and salt and pepper.
- Blend for 1 minute on high. The sauce will seem really thin. No worries, it will thicken as it cooks in the following step.
- Place in a saucepan, turn heat to the lowest possible setting and cook for 10-15 minutes, until sauce becomes bubbly. Turn off heat.

Veggies

- Heat water for the pasta while you make the veggies (follow directions on the pasta box).
- Heat the olive oil in a skillet and saute the onions for 5 minutes on medium - low.
- Add mushrooms and cook for an additional 2 minutes.
- Add kale, stir to incorporate and cook for 2 minutes.
- Add salt and pepper and give it a final stir.

Assemble

- Place a portion of the noodles on each plate.
- Pour white sauce over pasta and top with veggies.
- Garnish with parsley.

Pizza

Makes two 12 inch pizzas
Time: 30 plus minutes
Difficulty Level: 5 over 5 (but so totally worth it!)
Additional recipe required
Cashew cheese, page 83
Red sauce, page 83
SF Soy free

DIFFICULTY
5/5
LEVEL

stuff you need...

Crust (makes two 12 inch crusts)

1 1/2 cups warm water
2 teaspoon active yeast (8g)
1 teaspoon sugar (6g)
4 cups plain white flour (600g)
1 teaspoon salt (6g)
1/3 cup olive oil (80ml)
extra oil for brushing
extra flour for dusting

directions

turn the page for toppings, cashew cheese and red sauce

- Place warm water in a bowl, add sugar and yeast and mix together.
- Set aside for 5 -15 minutes, until frothy.
- In a separate large bowl add flour and salt and make a hole in the middle.
- Pour olive oil and yeast mixture into hole and mix together.
- Bring dough together in a ball and knead for 15 minutes on a floured work surface.
- Drizzle a little olive oil on the ball and spread it around to coat the entire ball.
- Cut dough in half so that you have two equal size balls.
- Wrap in food grade plastic so no air can get in and place in fridge overnight.
- Take pizza dough out of the fridge two hours before you want to make the pizza.
- Immediately after you take out of the fridge, take dough balls out of the plastic and set them on a floured baking sheet.
- Spread a little olive oil on them and cover with a clean kitchen towel. Allow to sit in a warm area for 2 hours (check on them after an hour and if it looks like they are drying out add more olive oil).
- Preheat oven to 400°F (205°C) with the pizza stone in the oven for at least 30 minutes.
- After two hours, punch the dough down and let rest for 10 additional minutes.
- Flour a work surface and roll out the dough with a rolling pin until you have a 12 inch circle, about 1/2 inch thick.
- Place the dough on the heated pizza stone and top with sauce and toppings.
- Place in the oven for 12-15 minutes.

continued from the pizza crust

Red Sauce

Make the red sauce recipe on page 83 and allow it to cool for 10 minutes. After 10 minutes, place it in a food processor or blender and process/blend until you reach a desired consistency.

Topping Idea

red sauce (page 83)
2 tablespoons olive oil (60ml)
1 onion, diced (190g)
6 large garlic cloves, sliced
2 very large portobello mushroom, diced into large squares, stems and all (370g)
3 cups kale, thinly sliced (90g)
1/2 teaspoon salt (3g)
1 tablespoon dried basil (4g)
4 tomatoes, sliced
1 recipe cashew cheese (page 83)

- Heat olive oil in a skillet and saute onions for 5 minutes, stirring occasionally until just brown.
- Add garlic and mushrooms and a sprinkle of salt. Cook for 2 minutes and then drizzle 2 tablespoons (30ml) of water over the mixture, cover with a lid and cook for an additional minute.
- Add kale, salt and dried basil, stir and turn off heat.
- Once the pizza crust is on the heated stone, top with the red sauce, followed by the onion/mushroom/kale mixture.
- Next, arrange the tomatoes evenly over the pizza and top with the cashew cheese (dollop mounds of the cheese evenly over the pizza).
- Brush the crust with olive oil and pop in the oven for 12-15 minutes.

cook's notes

· Once you have a good crust, the rest is easy peasy and you can top it with whatever you want or have on hand. Maybe cashew cheese, roasted eggplant, vegan sausage, fresh spinach, caramelized onions and sauteed mushrooms.
Or keep it simple.
Perhaps fresh basil, tempeh bacon, tomato slices and roasted butternut squash. Use your imagination and run wild.
· You can't go wrong with the toppings, have fun with it and enjoy the creative process of making your own pizza.

Cashew Cheese

Time: 30 plus minutes (this is because the cashews need to soak. Once the cashews are soaked it will take about 10 minutes).

Makes 1 cup / 210g
 Gluten free
Soy free

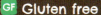 stuff you need...

1 cup cashews (130g) soaked in 3 cups (709 ml) of water for at least 1 hour.
2 teaspoons lemon juice (10ml)
1/2 teaspoon salt (3g)
2 turns fresh black pepper
1/4 cup water (60ml)

directions

- Soak, drain and rinse cashews.
- Place in a food processor, along with lemon juice, salt and black pepper.
- Pulse for about 1 minute to combine ingredients.
- Add water and process until completely smooth, about 2-4 minutes.

 cook's notes

· You can soak the cashews up to overnight. The longer you soak them the creamier the final product will be.
· You may want to turn off the food processor and scrape down the cheese from the sides a couple of times.
· Think of this as a base recipe. From here, you can add chives, garlic, rosemary, whatever you want to make it fancy.

Red Sauce

Time: 15 - 30 minutes

Makes 4 1/2 cups / 1.2kg
GF Gluten free
NF Nut free
SF Soy free

 stuff you need...

3 tablespoons olive oil
1 yellow onion, diced (245g)
6 garlic cloves, minced
3 cups mushrooms, sliced (200g)
7 roma tomatoes, diced (450g)
2 tablespoons tomato paste (40g)
1 can tomato sauce (15oz / 426g)
1 bunch fresh basil leaves, chopped (30g)
1/2 tablespoon dried oregano (2g)
1/2 tablespoon dried basil (2g)
1 teaspoon sea salt (6g)
1 tablespoon sugar (15g)

directions

- Heat olive oil in a large pot and saute the onions and garlic for 3 minutes.
- Add the mushrooms and cook for 3 additional minutes.
- Add tomatoes, tomato paste, tomato sauce, fresh basil, dried oregano, dried basil, salt and sugar.
- Simmer on low for 20 minutes.

 cook's notes

· If you make the sauce a day in advance, the flavors will be more pronounced and delicious.

Veggie Pot Pie

DIFFICULTY 4½/5 LEVEL

Time: 30 plus minutes
(including pie crust recipe)
Additional recipe required:
pie crust page 196
Makes 1 pie / serves 4-6

GF Gluten free if making the gluten free pie crust recipe

NF Nut free

SF Soy free if using soy free Earth Balance buttery spread

Filling

1 tablespoon Earth Balance buttery spread (15g)

1 tablespoon olive oil (15g)

1 medium yellow onion, diced (120g)

4 celery stalks, diced (120g)

1 cup carrot, diced (140g)

4 cups mushrooms, cut into 1 inch chunks (235g)

2 cups broccoli florets, cut into small, bite-sized pieces (100g)

2 cups vegan chicken broth (475ml)

1 tablespoon tomato paste (20g)

1 cup firm tofu, cut into 1/2 inch cubes (170g)

1/2 cup parsley, chopped (12g)

4 tablespoons rice flour (40g)

1/2 teaspoon thyme

1/2 teaspoon salt (3g)

10 turns fresh black pepper

1 teaspoon garlic powder (4g)

1/2 cup frozen peas (60g)

directions

Filling

- Heat Earth Balance and olive oil in a medium-sized pan.
- Add onions, celery and carrot and cook for 2 minutes, stirring once or twice.
- Add mushroom, broccoli and the vegan chicken broth, cover pan with lid, turn to medium/low and cook for 5 minutes.
- Add tomato paste and stir.
- Add tofu and parsley and cook for 2 minutes.
- Add flour, thyme, salt, pepper and garlic powder.
- Stir until all ingredients are combined and mixture is thick.
- Add peas, stir mixture and turn off heat.

Choose pie crust recipe from page 196, make it and come back here!

Choose pie crust recipe from page 196, make it and come back here!

- Heat oven to 425°F (220°C)
- Take the dough balls from the fridge and place one of the balls on a floured work surface.
- Sprinkle some flour on top of the ball and on a rolling pin.
- Gently roll the dough out, turning clockwise after every other roll until the dough is a 1/4 inch thick circle.
- Lightly grease a 9-inch round glass pie pan.
- Place the rolled out dough in the bottom of the pan by folding it in half and gently placing in the pie pan and unfolding. Press the crust into the pie pan, bringing up the edges so that a bit of the crust hangs over the pie pan.
- Spread the filling evenly on the bottom crust.
- Roll out the second dough ball and place on top of the filling.
- Pinch the edge of the bottom crust and the edge of the top crust together, going around the whole pie so that the edges are sealed.
- Using a knife, make a few short slits in the top of the pie.
- Gently spread a bit of olive oil on the top crust and bake for 30-35 minutes.

cook's notes

· Any variety of mushroom will do. If you are making a gluten free crust you may have to do a bit of patchwork.

· The absence of gluten makes it a little harder to work with but still totally doable.

· Just have patience and piece together the crust as needed.

Green Chili Cheese Enchiladas

DIFFICULTY
4/5
LEVEL

Time: 30 plus minutes (Including cheese and green chili sauce recipes)

Additional recipe required:
Cheese sauce, page 192
Green chili sauce, page 198

Serves 6 - 10

GF Gluten free if using gluten free corn tortillas and if you swap out the Gardein chicken with sauteed mushrooms.

NF Nut free

SF Soy free if making the cheese sauce soy free and if you swap out the Gardein chicken with sauteed mushrooms.

I'm Hungry! (main meals)

stuff you need...

1 recipe (3 cups / 700g) cheese sauce (page 192)
1 recipe (3 1/2 cup / 870g) green chili sauce (198)
1 package frozen Gardein vegan Teriyaki chicken strips (use without the sauce)
1 cup frozen corn (130g)
23 corn tortillas
1 cup Daiya cheese, Cheddar style (20g)

directions

- Preheat the oven to 350°F (175°C)
- In a 9x13" pan, place 1/2 cup (115g) of the green chili sauce on the bottom of the pan and spread around, evenly.
- Place 6 corn tortillas evenly over the green chili (see cook's notes).
- On top of the tortillas, evenly place 12 frozen Gardein chicken strips.
- Place 1/2 cup (65g) of corn evenly over the chicken.
- Evenly distribute 1 cup (230g) of green chili sauce over the corn.
- Place 2/3 cup (155g) of cheese sauce over the green chili.

  "Layer the rest of this dish in the following order, making sure to evenly distribute"
- 6 corn tortillas
- 6 Gardein chicken strips
- 1/2 cup green chili (115g)
- 2/3 cup cheese sauce (155g)
- 1/2 cup corn (65g)
- 6 corn tortillas
- 6 Gardein chicken strips
- 1/2 cup green chili sauce (115g)
- 1/2 cup cheese sauce (120g)
- 6 tortillas
- remaining chili sauce
- remaining cheese sauce
- 1 cup Daiya cheese
- Cover with tinfoil and bake for 45 - 50 minutes

cook's notes

· Place the tortillas so that they just touch each other in the middle of the pan. With kitchen scissors, cut off the excess tortilla that will be hanging over the edge of the pan. This will make an even layer of tortilla so that there will not be a thick middle part of your casserole. You can use the excess tortilla in the scrambled tortilla recipe (page 64).

· If you don't want to use the Gardein chicken you can swap it out with sauteed mushrooms.

· If you do use the strips then keep the Teriyaki sauce and use it at a later time on veggies or tofu.

· You can make the cheese sauce and green chili sauce a day or two in advance to cut down on time.

Time: 15-30 minutes
Difficulty Level: 3 over 5

Serves 2-3
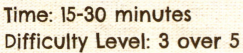 Gluten free if using gluten free soy sauce
NF Nut free

I'm Hungry! (main meals)

Korean Glass Noodles with Mushrooms, Green Onions and Sesame (Chap Jae)

stuff you need...

6 cups water (1.5 liters)
3 portions mung bean noodles
2 tablespoons grapeseed oil (30ml)
1 red onion cut in half and then cut into 1/4 inch half rings (210g)
4 large garlic cloves, peeled and minced
2 cups crimini mushrooms, sliced (120g)
1 cup carrots, sliced into ribbons with a vegetable slicer (50g)
5 green onions, cut into 1 - 1 1/2 inch pieces - use green parts only.
2 cups spinach leaves, left whole (70g)
2 teaspoons sesame oil, divided (30ml)
1/4 cup soy sauce (60ml)
1/2 teaspoon sugar (3g)
Sprinkle of white pepper
Sprinkle of sesame seeds

directions

- Bring 6 cups of water to a boil.
- Add mung bean noodles to the pan and cook covered for 4 minutes.
- Rinse, strain and pour back into the pan.
- Drizzle noodles with 1 teaspoon (5ml) sesame oil and set aside.
- Heat the grapeseed oil in a large non-stick skillet on medium heat.
- Add onions and garlic and cook for 3 minutes.
- Add mushrooms, stir and saute for 1 minute.
- Add carrots and green onions. Cook for 30 seconds.
- Pour 2 tablespoons of water (30ml) over the veggies, cover the pan with a lid and cook for 1 minute.
- Add the noodles, spinach, remaining 1 teaspoon (5ml) sesame oil, soy sauce and sugar.
- Gently stir everything so that the ingredients are incorporated and cook for 4 minutes.
- Sprinkle with white pepper and sesame seeds before serving.

cook's notes

· If you are unfamiliar with mung bean noodles, please refer to page 9 to read all about them.
· The noodles will fall apart unless you are gentle with them. We recommend using a pasta fork and a chopstick to stir.

Sesame Tofu Rice Bowl
with Swiss Chard

Time: 30 plus minutes (including additional required recipe)

Additional recipe required:
    Stovetop Cilantro Rice page 194

Serves 3

GF Gluten free if using gluten free soy sauce
NF Nut free

DIFFICULTY 2½/5 LEVEL

I'm Hungry! (main meals)

stuff you need...

directions

2 cups firm tofu, cut into small bite-sized pieces (260g)
1 tablespoon olive oil (15ml)
4 cloves garlic, minced
1 tablespoon peeled and minced ginger (10g)
2 green onions, chopped. Use all of the onion except for the stem.
5 swiss chard leaves, thinly sliced, including the stems. (160g)
1/4 teaspoon sea salt (2g)
1/4 teaspoon white pepper
1 teaspoon sesame seeds (4g)
1 recipe Stovetop Cilantro Rice, heated (page 194)

Tofu Marinade

2 teaspoons sesame oil (10ml)
1 tablespoon mirin (15ml)
2 tablespoons soy sauce (30ml)

- Marinate the tofu for at least 10 minutes (up to overnight) by mixing all of the sauce ingredients together and pouring it over the tofu in a bowl.
- When the tofu is done marinating heat the olive oil in a skillet and add the garlic, ginger and green onions. Cook for 2 minutes over medium
- heat.
  Add the tofu (along with the mari-
- nade) and cook for 5 - 10 minutes, stirring frequently so that all sides of the tofu get brown.
  Add the chard, sea salt and white pepper and cook for 2 additional
- minutes.
  Turn off heat.
  To serve, place 1 cup of rice in each
- bowl (140g), topped with 1 cup of
- tofu/chard mixture (110g), followed by 1 teaspoon of sesame seeds (4g)

· A non-stick skillet works best for this recipe.
· This recipe is on the simple side as far as taste. If you want to add more zing, feel free to add in some red pepper flakes or additional seasonings into the marinade.

cook's notes

Slow Cooker Squash Lasagna

DIFFICULTY 3/5 LEVEL

Time: 30 plus minutes (including cheese sauce recipe. Take note that this dish gets cooked in the slow cooker for 3 hours)

Additional recipe required:
    Cheese sauce page 192

Serves 6-8

GF Gluten free if using gluten free lasagna noodles
NF Nut free
SF Soy free

stuff you need...

1 head cauliflower, cut into small, bite-sized pieces (4 cups / 400g)

3 1/2 cups winter squash, diced into small bite-sized pieces (470g)

1 tablespoon olive oil (15ml)

1 teaspoon sage

10 turns fresh black pepper

1/2 teaspoon salt (3g)

1/2 cup parsley, chopped (25g)

5 cups mushrooms, sliced (330g)

1 recipe cheese sauce (3 cups / 700g) page 192

1 box lasagna noodles

directions

- Place 1/2 cup (120g) of cheese sauce on the bottom of the crock pot. Followed by
- 3 lasagna noodles (you can break to fit)
- 1/2 cup cheese sauce (120g)
- 1/2 of the cauliflower
- 1/3 of the mushrooms
- 1/3 of the squash
- 1/3 of the parsley
- 1/2 cup cheese sauce (120g)
- 3 noodles (again, break to fit)
- Remaining cauliflower
- 1/3 of the mushrooms
- 1/3 of the squash
- 1/3 of the parsley
- 1/2 cup cheese sauce (120g)
- 3 noodles (again, break to fit)
- Remaining mushrooms
- Remaining squash
- Remaining parsley
- Remaining cheese sauce
- Cover slow cooker and cook on low for 3 hours.

cook's notes

· Winter Squash includes all hard squash such as Acorn, Delicata, Turban, Butternut, Kabocha and Hubbard to name a few.
· You can use any variety of lasagna as long as you do not pre-cook the noodles.

Time: 5 - 15 minutes (does not include
Anasazi beans and green chili sauce)
Additional recipe required:
      Anasazi beans page 202
      Green chili sauce page 198

Serves 1

NF Nut free

SF Soy free if you omit the vegan sour
cream (or find a soy free version)

Anasazi Bean Burrito with Avocado smothered in Green Chili *Sauce*

directions

stuff you need...

1 whole wheat tortilla
1 cup Anasazi beans (240g) recipe page 202
1 cup green chili sauce (230) recipe page 198
1/2 avocado, sliced
1 dollop vegan sour cream

- Heat tortilla and place beans in the middle.
- Roll up and smother with green chili sauce.
- Top with sour cream and place the avocado on the side.

cook's notes

· I use vegan sour cream by Follow Your Heart
· This recipe is super easy once you make the beans and the green chili sauce. If you don't have time to make those recipes, just buy store bought beans and chili sauce.

Ginger Soy Steamed Tofu in Parchment Paper

DIFFICULTY **3/5** LEVEL

Time: 15 - 30 minutes
Serves 2

GF Gluten free
NF Nut free

I'm Hungry! (main meals)

stuff you need...

1 package firm tofu (14oz. 397g)

1 green onion, use white part only and cut into thin strips (see picture)

1/2 large tomato, diced (80g)

1/2 cup cilantro, coarsely chopped (6g)

5 turns fresh black pepper

Sauce

1/4 cup soy sauce (60ml)

1 teaspoon mirin (5ml)

1 teaspoon rice vinegar (5ml)

2 teaspoons lime juice (10ml)

1/2 teaspoon sesame oil (2.5ml)

1/2 teaspoon brown sugar (4g)

2 teaspoons finely minced ginger (8g)

2 tablespoons water (30ml)

cook's notes

· The tofu is meant to be soft, similar to South East Asian steamed fish.

· Serve dish with the package closed so that your guest can open it themselves.

directions

- Preheat oven to 375°F (190°C).
- Cut the tofu in half lengthwise so that you have two portions.
- Cut slits into each half, being careful not to cut all the way through. Do this horizontally and then vertically so that you have cubes that are still intact (see pictures).
- In an 8x8 baking dish place two portions of parchment paper side by side so that there is enough overlap of paper to wrap each portion of tofu like a package (see pictures).
- Place the tofu in parchment paper (see pictures).
- Make sauce by placing all of the sauce ingredients into a small bowl and mixing to combine.
- Divide sauce evenly over both portions of tofu.
- Top with green onion, tomato, cilantro and black pepper and wrap the tofu so that it is totally enclosed.
- Bake for 20 minutes.
- Place each package of tofu in a bowl with the parchment paper.
- Serve with rice (page 194).

Food for the Body & Soul

Farfalle (bowtie) Pasta with Balsamic Vinegar, Asparagus and Cherry Tomatoes

Time: 5 - 15 minutes
Serves 4

SF Soy free

DIFFICULTY
1½/5
LEVEL

I'm Hungry! (main meals)

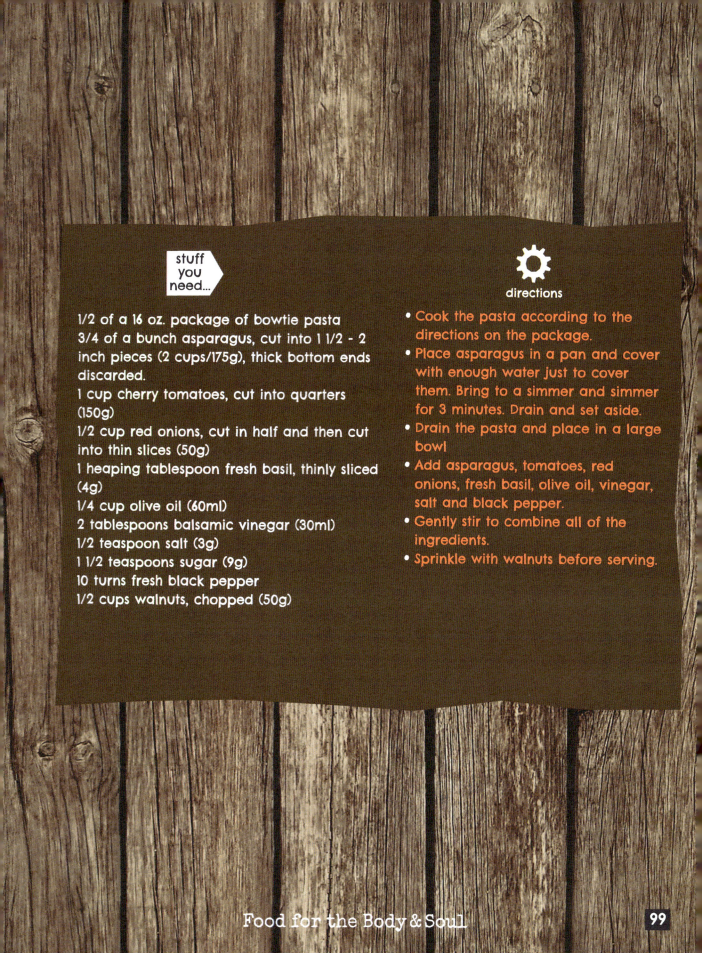

stuff you need...

1/2 of a 16 oz. package of bowtie pasta
3/4 of a bunch asparagus, cut into 1 1/2 - 2 inch pieces (2 cups/175g), thick bottom ends discarded.
1 cup cherry tomatoes, cut into quarters (150g)
1/2 cup red onions, cut in half and then cut into thin slices (50g)
1 heaping tablespoon fresh basil, thinly sliced (4g)
1/4 cup olive oil (60ml)
2 tablespoons balsamic vinegar (30ml)
1/2 teaspoon salt (3g)
1 1/2 teaspoons sugar (9g)
10 turns fresh black pepper
1/2 cups walnuts, chopped (50g)

directions

- Cook the pasta according to the directions on the package.
- Place asparagus in a pan and cover with enough water just to cover them. Bring to a simmer and simmer for 3 minutes. Drain and set aside.
- Drain the pasta and place in a large bowl
- Add asparagus, tomatoes, red onions, fresh basil, olive oil, vinegar, salt and black pepper.
- Gently stir to combine all of the ingredients.
- Sprinkle with walnuts before serving.

Food for the Body & Soul

A Little Extra Love on the Side
(salads, sides and dips)

Beet, ginger and sesame Salad

DIFFICULTY 2½/5 LEVEL

Time: 15 - 30 minutes
Serves 4

GF Gluten free if using gluten free soy sauce
SF Soy free if you omit the soy sauce and are
using soy free Earth Balance buttery spread

1/2 large beet, grated (1 cup / 100g)
1 large carrot, grated (2 cups / 165g)
1/2 cup parsley, chopped (10g)
1/4 cup sesame seeds (35g)
1/2 cup sunflower seeds (70g)
3 garlic cloves, sliced
1 tablespoon Earth Balance buttery spread (15g)

Sauce

1 tablespoon sesame oil (15ml)
2 teaspoons soy sauce (10ml)
Juice from 1/2 lime
1/4 teaspoon 5 spice powder
1/2 teaspoon ginger, peeled and grated (4g)
1/2 teaspoon sugar (2g)

directions

- Make the sauce by adding all of the sauce ingredients into a small bowl and whisk to combine. Set aside.
- In a large bowl, add the beet, carrot and parsley and set aside.
- Heat a medium-sized skillet for 1 minute and add the sesame seeds and sunflower seeds. The pan should be dry, no oil or butter.
- Let cook for 3 minutes on medium/low heat, stirring frequently so that they won't burn.
- Turn off heat and add seeds to the beet and carrots.
- In the same skillet, heat the Earth Balance.
- Add the garlic and cook for 3 minutes on medium/low, stirring frequently as to not to burn.
- Turn off heat and add the garlic (along with the butter in the pan) to the beet/carrot bowl.
- Add the sauce to the bowl and stir to combine.

cook's notes

· If you opt for the soy free version, leave out the soy sauce and add salt to taste.

Time: 5 - 15 minutes
Serves 4 as a side

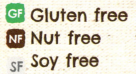 Gluten free
 Nut free
SF Soy free

DIFFICULTY
1½
/5
LEVEL

A Little Extra Love on the Side (salads, sides and dips)

Creamy Coleslaw

directions

stuff you need...

1/2 small head green cabbage, shredded (310g)

1 medium carrot, grated (110g)

1/2 red onion, thinly sliced (70g)

Sauce

3/4 cup vegan mayo (180g)

1 teaspoon apple cider vinegar (5ml)

2 teaspoons sugar (10g)

- Place veggies into a large mixing bowl.
- Make sauce by combining all of the sauce ingredients into a small bowl.
- Pour sauce over veggies and stir until thoroughly combined.

cook's notes

· If you have a food processor you can use the grating tool for the carrot and the shredding tool for cabbage and red onion. This will cut the prep time in half.

· We use vegan mayo by Vegenaise.

Ginger and Garlic Stir Fried Green Beans

Time: 5 - 15 minutes
Serves 2-3

GF Gluten free

NF Nut free

SF Soy free is using soy free Earth Balance buttery spread

A Little Extra Love on the Side (salads, sides and dips)

DIFFICULTY 1½/5 LEVEL

1 tablespoon olive oil (15ml)
1 teaspoon Earth Balance buttery spread (6g)
7 garlic cloves, peeled and thinly sliced
2 green onions, thinly sliced, discard the bottom end (12g)
1 teaspoon ginger, peeled and minced (4g)
2 1/2 cups green beans, destemmed and cut into 1 1/2 inch long pieces (230g)
1/4 teaspoon salt (2g)
1 tablespoon water (15ml)

directions

- Heat olive oil and Earth Balance in a skillet on medium heat.
- Add the garlic and cook for 3 minutes until it turns golden brown, stirring occasionally.
- Add green onions and cook for 30 seconds.
- Add ginger and cook for an additional 30 seconds.
- Add green beans to the pan and turn the heat to high.
- Cook for 4 minutes.
- Add the salt and 1 tablespoon of water, stir and cover the pan.
- Cook for 1 minute.
- Serve.

cook's notes

· The green beans in this recipe come out slightly crunchy. If you like your beans less crunchy, cook them for an additional 2 or 3 minutes prior to covering them with a lid.

Teriyaki Pan Fried Tofu

Time: 15-30 minutes
Serves 4 as an appetizer

GF Gluten free if using gluten free soy sauce
NF Nut free

A Little Extra Love on the Side (salads, sides and dips)

stuff you need...

1 14 oz. package firm tofu cut into 2 inch x 1 inch domino shaped rectangles, 1/4 - 1/2 inch thick (460g)

1 tablespoon Earth Balance buttery spread (15g)

1/2 cup shallots, sliced into thin rounds (45g)

1/4 cup chopped green onions, discard bottom end (20g)

1 tablespoon grapeseed oil (15ml)

Sauce

1/4 cup soy sauce (60ml)

1 tablespoon brown sugar (15g)

1 teaspoon sesame oil (5ml)

1 teaspoon mirin (5ml)

3 tablespoons water (45ml)

1 teaspoon lime juice (5ml)

1 garlic clove, peeled and grated

1/2 teaspoon peeled and grated ginger (2g)

directions

- Make sauce by mixing all of the sauce ingredients together.
- In a large bowl, marinate tofu in the sauce for at least 10 minutes.
- Heat Earth Balance in a small skillet over medium/low heat.
- Add shallots and green onions and cook for 6 minutes, until golden brown. Stir frequently.
- Turn off heat and drain shallots on a paper bag and set aside.
- Heat grapeseed oil in a large skillet over medium heat.
- Remove tofu from sauce and pan fry it for 4 minutes on each side (keep sauce and set it aside).
- Pour in the leftover sauce and cook for an additional 2 minutes.
- Place tofu squares on a plate and sprinkle the shallots and green onions over it.

cook's notes

· Serve by itself as an appetizer, with fried rice (page 128) or as a side dish.

Time: 15 - 30 minutes
Serves 4-6

GF Gluten free if using gluten free pasta
NF Nut free
SF Soy free if using soy free Earth Balance buttery spread

A Little Extra Love on the Side (salads, sides and dips)

Creamy Mac & Cheese

1 russet potato, peeled and cut into bite-sized pieces (1 1/2 cups/ 240g)
1 cup carrot, cut into 1/2 inch rounds (130g)
1/4 yellow onion, diced (1/2 cup/ 65g)
2 cups water (16 oz.)
1/2 cup Earth Balance buttery spread (70g)
1/2 cup nutritional yeast (40g)
1/2 teaspoon turmeric
1 teaspoon salt (6g)
3 tablespoons coconut milk (1 1/2 oz.)
3 turns fresh black pepper

1 box (8 oz. / 227g) regular or gluten free pasta (Garden Pagodas quinoa pasta by Ancient Harvest is my fave).
Parsley for garnish

cook's notes

· It will seem like a lot of cheese sauce compared to pasta. The pasta absorbs quite a lot of sauce so I like to err on the side of too much sauce rather than too little.

directions

Cheese Sauce

- Place potato, carrot and onion in a pan, cover with 2 cups of water and
- simmer for 20 minutes with the lid on.
- After 20 minutes, turn off heat and add Earth Balance, nutritional yeast, turmeric and salt. Stir to combine until melted.
- Pour mixture into a blender and blend until creamy and smooth, about a minute on medium. You may need to scrape the sides down from the blender a couple of times for everything to get incorporated.
- Add coconut milk to the blender and continue to blend until mixture is creamy throughout.
- Leave in the blender for now.

Pasta

- Cook pasta according to the directions on the box.
- Strain pasta and rinse with cold water to stop from cooking. Return to pan.
- Turn heat on very low and pour cheese sauce over pasta.
- Add black pepper and stir to combine.
- Turn off heat and serve.
- Garnish with parsley.

Roasted Root Veggies

Time: 15 - 30 minutes
Serves 4-6

GF Gluten free
NF Nut free
SF Soy free

DIFFICULTY
2/5
LEVEL

stuff you need...

2 turnips, peeled and cut into 1 inch bite-sized chunks (450g)

1 rutabaga, peeled and cut into 1 inch bite-sized chunks (335g)

1 sweet potato, cut into 1 inch bite-sized chunks (310g)

1/2 red onion, cut into 2 inch chunks (160g)

3 tablespoons olive oil (45ml)

1 teaspoon salt (6g)

10 turns fresh ground black pepper

directions

- Preheat oven to 425°F (220°C).
- Place all of the cut up veggies in a large bowl.
- Pour in the olive oil and add the salt and pepper.
- Stir well so that all of the veggies are coated with oil and seasonings.
- Place in the oven and cook for 15 minutes.
- Take out of the oven and stir the veggies.
- Put back in the oven and cook for an additional 20-25 minutes, until veggies are soft and slightly brown on the edges.

Baked Kale Chips-3 ways

DIFFICULTY
4½/5
LEVEL

Time: 30 plus minutes

GF Gluten free
NF Soy free
SF Nut free

A Little Extra Love on the Side (salads, sides and dips)

3 bunches of dino or curly kale
Flavor of your choice (see below)

directions

- Thoroughly wash the kale and take the stems off from each leaf. You can either cut it out with a knife or pull it off with your hands. To do the hand method, grab the stem at the base of the leaf and pull up toward the top of the leaf, while holding on to the stem.
- Leave the kale in as big of pieces as possible.
- They will shrink slightly as well as break a bit so the bigger the better when they go in the oven.
- Dry the kale. This step is super important because if the kale is wet or damp, the chips will not get as crispy as they do when they are dried thoroughly. To dry the kale you can spin it in a salad spinner and then lay flat to dry on clean kitchen towels. If you don't have a salad spinner then just lay the kale on clean kitchen towels and wait until both sides are dry, about 30 minutes.
- Choose a flavor for your chips (see ideas below) and preheat oven to 300°F (150°C).
- In a large bowl, place the washed, de-stemmed and dried kale.
- In a small bowl, mix together the ingredients of the flavor you desire until ingredients are combined.
- Pour the mixture over the kale and use your hands to massage it into the leaves. Make sure that all parts of the kale are covered with the mixture.
- Line two baking sheets with parchment paper and place kale on the sheets in a single layer and bake for 5 minutes (10 if using curly kale).
- Turn over and bake for 5 additional minutes (10 if using curly kale) or until kale is crisp but not burned.
- Take out and lay flat to cool.
- Repeat until all of the kale has been baked.

Flavor Ideas

Agave Mustard
1 tablespoon agave nectar (15ml)
1 tablespoon yellow mustard (20g)
1/2 teaspoon olive oil (2.5ml) or 1 teaspoon (5ml) if using curly kale
1/8 teaspoon sea salt

Garlicky Sea Salt
1/2 teaspoon sea salt (3g)
1 teaspoon garlic granules (4g)
1 tablespoon olive oil (15ml) or 2 tablespoons (30ml) if using curly kale.

Nacho Cheese
1/2 cup nutritional yeast (40g)
1 teaspoon paprika
2 teaspoons red chili powder (6g)
1/2 teaspoon sea salt (3g)
1 tablespoon olive oil (15ml) or 2 tablespoons (30ml) if using curly kale.

De-stem

Drying

Spice it up!

Time: 5 - 15 minutes after the cashews
have been soaked overnight.
Makes 2 1/4 cup / 530g

DIFFICULTY
1½
/
5
LEVEL

GF Gluten free
SF Soy free

A Little Extra Love on the Side (salads, sides and dips)

Toasted Cumin and Lime Cashew Dip

stuff you need...

2 cups raw cashews (275g), soaked overnight in 5 cups of water
1 tablespoon olive oil (15ml)
2 teaspoons cumin seeds (6g)
1/4 cup lime juice (60ml)
1/2 cup of water (120ml)
1/4 cup cilantro, stems and leaves (8g)
1 teaspoon salt (6g)
1/2 teaspoon sugar (4g)

directions

- Drain and rinse cashews and place them in a food processor.
- Heat oil in a small skillet and add cumin seeds.
- Cook for 1 minutes on low heat, stirring constantly so they do not burn.
- Immediately add them to the cashews along with lime juice, water, cilantro, salt and sugar.
- Process until completely smooth, about 3 minutes, stopping a couple of times to scrape down the edges so that everything gets incorporated.

Creamy Macaroni Salad

DIFFICULTY 2½/5 **LEVEL**

Time: 15 - 30 minutes
This dish is large enough to bring to a large potluck

NF Nut free
SF Soy free if using soy free Vegenaise

stuff you need...

3 cups uncooked elbow pasta (315g)
1/2 red onion, diced (85g)
6 celery stalks, diced (2 1/2 cups/300g)
1/4 cup parsley, chopped (15g)

Sauce
1 3/4 cups Vegenaise (350g)
1 tablespoon apple cider vinegar
1 teaspoon celery powder (2g)
1/2 teaspoon dried dill
1 tablespoon sugar (15g)
1/2 teaspoon salt (4g)
1/4 cup nutritional yeast (15g)
7 turns fresh black pepper

directions

- Bring 9 cups of water to a boil.
- Add pasta and cook for about 10 minutes or until they are done (you want them slightly al dente. Check the box, different pasta may call for different cooking times).
- While the pasta is cooking, chop the onions, celery and parsley and set aside.
- Make the sauce by adding all of the sauce ingredients into a bowl and whisking to incorporate.
- When pasta is done cooking, drain the water, rinse with cold water and strain. Let pasta dry for 10 minutes. If it is wet, then it will affect the overall consistency of the dish.
- Place pasta in a large mixing bowl.
- Add onions, celery and parsley. Stir.
- Add the sauce and stir so that all ingredients are mixed together.

Mushroom Walnut Pate

DIFFICULTY
2/5
LEVEL

Time: 15 - 30 minutes
Serves 4 -6 as an appetizer

GF Gluten free if using gluten free soy sauce and you serve it with gluten free crackers or gluten free bread
SF Soy free if you omit the soy sauce

A Little Extra Love on the Side (salads, sides and dips)

2 cups walnuts (180g)
1 tablespoon olive oil (15ml)
1 medium red onion, chopped (1 1/4 cup /160g)
4 garlic cloves, minced
1 teaspoon peeled and grated ginger (6g)
2 cups mushrooms, sliced (145g)
1/2 teaspoon dried tarragon
1/4 cup water (60ml)
1/2 cup parsley, loosely packed (6g)
1 teaspoon balsamic vinegar (5ml)
1 teaspoon soy sauce (5ml)
1/2 teaspoon salt (3g)
5 turns black pepper

directions

- In a skillet (preferably, cast iron) dry toast the walnuts (leave them whole) for **6 minutes** on low heat, stirring occasionally. Turn off heat and set aside.
- Heat the olive oil in a separate large skillet over medium heat and add the onions, ginger and garlic. Cook for **3 minutes**.
- Add mushrooms and tarragon and cook for an additional minute.
- Add the water, cover the skillet, turn heat to low and cook for **2 minutes**. Turn off heat.
- Place the toasted walnuts, onion/mushroom mixture, parsley, vinegar, soy sauce, salt and black pepper in a food processor and process until smooth, for about **5 minutes**.
- Stop processing occasionally and use a rubber spatula to push down any pate that has collected on the side of the food processor. This will ensure a consistent texture.
- Chill for at least **3 hours**.
- Serve with crackers or toast points.

cook's notes

· If you omit the soy sauce you may need to add a bit more salt. Taste it when finished processing and adjust as needed.

Time: 30 plus minutes
Serves 6-8

GF Gluten free
NF Nut free
SF Soy free if you use a soy free vegan mayo

DIFFICULTY
2/5
LEVEL

Classic Potato Salad

directions

6 medium to large red potatoes, peeled and cut into quarters (2.5lb/1.10kg)

8 celery stalks, diced (2 cups/240g)

1/2 cup red onion, diced (55g)

Fresh parsley for garnish

Sauce

2 cups vegan mayo (440g)

2 teaspoons apple cider vinegar (10ml)

1 teaspoon celery powder (2g)

1 tablespoon onion powder (12g)

1 teaspoon dried dill

1 teaspoon sugar (6g)

1/2 teaspoon sea salt (3g)

5 or 6 turns fresh black pepper

cook's notes

· Use leafy green tops of the celery.

· I use Aioli vegan mayo by Wildwood for this recipe.

· If you don't allow the potatoes to cool, the dressing will get thin and your potato salad will be on the watery side.

- Bring 12 cups of water to a boil in a large pot.
- Add the potatoes and cook until tender, 20-25 minutes. Do not over-cook the potatoes. You want them to be soft all the way through but not mushy or falling apart.
- While potatoes are cooking, chop the celery and onions and place them into a large mixing bowl and set aside.
- Make the sauce by adding all of the sauce ingredients into a separate, smaller mixing bowl and whisking until everything is combined.
- When the potatoes are done, drain them, using a colander. Do not rinse them with water. Allow to dry, about 5 minutes.
- When potatoes are dry, cut them into bite-sized pieces and put them into the bowl with the celery and onions.
- When the potatoes are cool, pour the dressing over them and mix to combine all of the ingredients.
- Garnish with fresh parsley.

Salad with Fennel, Cranberries, garbanzo beans, pecans and Balsamic Citrus Dressing

DIFFICULTY
1/5
LEVEL

Time: 5 - 15 minutes if you have the garbanzo beans ready
Serves 4 as a side or 2 as main dish

GF Gluten free
SF Soy free

stuff you need...

3 cups romaine lettuce, chopped (130g)
1 cup fennel, thinly sliced (70g)
1/4 cup dried cranberries (30g)
1 cup cooked garbanzo beans
(recipe page 204) or canned (165g)
1/4 cup pecans, chopped (30g)
12 thin red onion rings

Dressing
Makes 1 1/2 cups / 355ml
Gluten free
Soy free
Nut free

1/4 cup balsamic vinegar (60ml)
Juice of 1 lemon
Juice of 2 oranges
1/2 cup olive oil (120)
2 tablespoon brown sugar (25g)
2 garlic cloves, grated
1/8 teaspoon sea salt

directions

- Place all dressing ingredients into a container with a lid, cover and shake well. Alternatively you can place all ingredients into a bowl and whisk to combine.
- Place all salad ingredients into a large bowl and toss to combine.
- Serve dressing on the side or toss it directly into the salad.

cook's notes

· You can use canned garbanzo beans if you don't have time to cook your own beans.

DIFFICULTY
1/5
LEVEL

Time: 5 - 15 minutes (does not include the baked tofu)

Additional recipe required
Sesame ginger baked tofu, page 190

Serves 4 as a side or 2 as main dish

GF Gluten free if using gluten free soy sauce

Kale, Romaine Salad w Baked Tofu, Avo, Walnuts, Raisins and Ginger Soy Dressing

stuff you need...

2 cups romaine, chopped (90g)
2 cups kale, thinly chopped (60g)
1 cup baked tofu, diced (recipe page 190) (120g)
1 avocado, sliced
1/3 cup walnuts, chopped (35g)
1/4 cup raisins (35g)

Dressing
Makes 1 cup/250ml
Gluten free
Nut free

1 heaping teaspoon, peeled and grated ginger (10g)
4 tablespoons soy sauce (60ml)
2 tablespoons mirin (30 ml)
4 tsp rice vinegar (20 ml)
1/2 cup olive oil (120ml)
1/2 tsp sugar (4g)

directions

- Place all dressing ingredients into a container with a lid, cover and shake well. Alternatively you can place all ingredients into a bowl and whisk to combine.
- Place all salad ingredients into a large bowl and toss to combine.
- Serve dressing on the side or toss it directly into the salad.

Time: 5 - 15 minutes
Serves 4

GF Gluten free if using gluten free soy sauce
NF Nut free

DIFFICULTY
2/5
LEVEL

A Little Extra Love on the Side (salads, sides and dips)

Fried Rice with Ginger Scallions and Mushrooms

stuff you need...

2 tablespoons grapeseed oil (30ml)
1 1/2 inch piece of ginger; about the size of a thumb, peeled and minced
4 garlic cloves, minced
1 medium carrot, diced (150g)
2 tablespoons water (30ml)
2 green onions, chopped into 1/4 inch pieces
3 tablespoons soy sauce, divided (45ml)
1/2 cup frozen green peas (70g)
2 portobello mushrooms, cut into 1 inch pieces (3 cups / 180g)
5 cups day old rice (680g)
1/4 teaspoon white pepper
Cilantro for garnish

- Heat oil in a large nonstick skillet.
- Add ginger and garlic and cook for 30 seconds.
- Add carrots and 2 tablespoons (30ml) of water.
- Cover pan with a lid and cook for 2 minutes.
- Take off lid, add green onions and 1 tablespoon (15ml) of the soy sauce and stir.
- Add peas and mushrooms and cook for 2 minutes.
- Add in the rice and stir to to combine all ingredients.
- Add remaining 2 tablespoons (30ml) of soy sauce and white pepper, stir and cook for 3 minutes.
- Garnish with cilantro

cook's notes

· Using day old rice is better because the rice will be dryer after it has sat overnight. Good fried rice is always dry, not wet.

· You can use any veggies that you have in your fridge.

The most crucial veggies are garlic, ginger and green onions.

Fresh Spring Rolls with Peanut Dipping Sauce

DIFFICULTY 4½/5 LEVEL

Time: 30 plus minutes
Makes 12 Spring Rolls

GF Gluten free if using gluten free soy sauce

A Little Extra Love on the Side (salads, sides and dips)

directions

12 rice paper wrappers
2 tablespoons grapeseed oil, divided (15g)
1 box firm tofu (12 oz. / 340g)
1 cucumber
2 cups bean sprouts, both ends plucked off (240g)
2 large portions dry glass noodles (140g)
1 cup mint, chopped (15g)
1 recipe of peanut dipping sauce (see next page)

Prepare all of the ingredients and set aside until ready to assemble.

Tofu

- Drain and rinse tofu and pat to dry with a clean kitchen cloth.
- Place on your cutting board and slice into 1/4 to 1/2 inch-thick, long strips (see picture). You should have about 45 strips when you are done.
- Heat 1 tablespoon of the oil in a non-stick pan and place half of the tofu in the pan. Cook on each side for 2 minutes or until golden brown.
- Sprinkle with salt and pepper and transfer to a plate.
- Heat the other tablespoon of oil in the pan and place the remaining tofu in the pan.
- Cook for 2 minutes on either side or until golden brown.
- Sprinkle with salt and pepper and place on the plate with the first batch of tofu.
- Set aside.

Cucumber

- Peel cucumber and slice lengthwise in half and scrape the seeds out with a spoon.
- Cut each side of the cucumber width-wise so you now have 4 pieces.
- Slice each piece into thin strips, about 1/4 inch thick.
- Place on a plate and set aside.

continue with recipe

Fresh Spring Rolls with Peanut Dipping Sauce

Bean Sprouts
- Place 2 cups (470ml) of water in a pan and bring to a boil.
- While waiting for the water to come to a boil, pluck off both ends of each bean sprout (Tedious? Yes! Worth it? Absolutely!).
- Place bean sprouts, sans ends in the water and cook for 30 seconds.
- Drain from water and set aside.

Glass Noodles / Mung Bean Noodles
- Cook the glass noodles per the direction on the package. If by chance the package is written in Chinese or another Asian language and you are left clueless, follow these directions:
- Bring 4 cups (945ml) of water to a boil.
- Add noodles and cook for 3 minutes.
- Drain and set aside.

Mint
- Chop and set aside.

Assemble
- Place 5 cups (1.2 liters) of warm water in a large bowl (larger than the rice wrappers).
- Place 1 wrapper at a time in the water and let soak for 2 minutes.
- Take the wrapper out of the bowl and place it on a cutting board.
- Layer the wrapper with the following ingredients, placing them in the middle of the wrapper:
  1 teaspoon mint
  1/4 cup cooked glass noodles (30g)
  3 cucumber slices
  3 tofu slices
  1/4 cup bean sprouts (30g)
- Fold like a burrito (see pictures)
- Allow to dry a few minutes and then cut in half.
- Repeat until ingredients are used up.
- Serve with peanut dipping sauce.

cook's notes
- This dish is on the tedious side but the end result is well worth the effort.
- You can make the dipping sauce a day in advance to cut down on prep time.

Peanut Dipping Sauce

Time: 5 - 15 minutes
Makes 2 1/2 cups / 535g

directions

GF Gluten free if using gluten free soy sauce

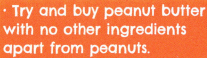
Place all ingredients into a food processor or blender and blend until completely smooth, about 2 minutes.

stuff you need...

1 cup smooth peanut butter, unsalted (250g)
3/4 cup coconut milk (175ml)
1 tablespoon lime juice (15ml)
2 tablespoons soy sauce (30ml)
2 teaspoons sesame oil (10ml)
1 tablespoon plus 1 teaspoon sugar (15g)
1 1/2 teaspoons, peeled and grated ginger (9g)
1/2 cup tightly packed cilantro stems and leaves (25g)
1/2 cup water plus 1 tablespoon (130ml)

cook's notes

· Try and buy peanut butter with no other ingredients apart from peanuts.
· If you have extra sauce and use it another day, you may need to thin it out by adding water and stirring.

Cauliflower and Cheese

Time: 30 plus minutes (including cheese sauce recipe)
Additional recipe required
Cheese sauce, page 192
Serves 4

GF Gluten free if using gluten free crackers
NF Nut free
SF Soy free if using soy free Earth Balance buttery spread in the cheese sauce

A Little Extra Love on the Side (salads, sides and dips)

stuff you need...

1 head cauliflower cut into florets (570g)
2 1/4 cups cheese sauce, (page 192) divided (520g)
1/4 cup crushed crackers (20g)
1 green onion, chopped (use green part only)
Fresh black pepper and sprinkle of sea salt

directions

- Preheat oven to 300°F (150°C).
- Cut and simmer cauliflower in 2 cups of water (475ml) for 10 minutes.
- Evenly spread 1/4 cup (60g) of cheese sauce on the bottom of a lightly oiled 8x8 baking pan.
- Add the cauliflower and sprinkle with several turns of fresh black pepper and a sprinkle of salt.
- Pour two cups (460g) of cheese sauce over the cauliflower and evenly top with crackers and green onions and bake for 20 minutes.

Time: 30 plus minutes
Makes 4 pancakes

NF Nut free

A Little Extra Love on the Side (salads, sides and dips)

Savory Green Onion Pancakes

Pancake Dough
1 1/3 cups all-purpose flour (215g)
½ teaspoon salt (3g)
2 teaspoons sugar (10g)
2 tablespoons Earth Balance buttery spread, melted (30g)
½ cup coconut milk (120ml)
1 teaspoon olive oil (5ml)

Filling
6 green onions, chopped. Use green parts only (1 1/4 cup / 55g).
2 teaspoons olive oil (10ml)
2 teaspoons sesame oil (10ml)
2 teaspoons white pepper
1/4 teaspoon salt

Dipping Sauce
2 tablespoons soy sauce (30ml)
1/2 teaspoon mirin (2.5ml)
1 teaspoon sesame (5ml)
3 tablespoons water (45ml)
1 clove garlic, minced
1/2 teaspoon peeled and grated ginger (4g)

directions

- Make dipping sauce by placing all of its ingredients into a bowl and whisking to combine. Set aside (see cook's notes for alternative dipping ideas).
- Add flour, salt and sugar into a large mixing bowl.
- Slowly add the melted Earth Balance and coconut milk and stir to combine.
- Knead dough for 10 minutes.
- Form dough into a ball and place into a bowl.
- Add 1 teaspoon of olive oil (5ml) over the ball and roll to coat with oil.
- Cover the bowl with a towel and set aside for 30 minutes.
- In a small bowl, place the filling ingredients; green onions, olive oil, sesame oil, white pepper and salt, stir and set aside.
- After the dough is done resting, cut into 4 equal pieces and lightly flour a clean work surface.
- Take one portion of the dough and roll into a thin circle. The circle should be so thin that it is nearly translucent.
- Place 1/4 of the filling, evenly onto the entire circle.
- Start from one end and roll it up like a thin burrito, making a point to roll it nice and tight (see picture).
- Take one end and coil it up like a snake until the entire thing is coiled (see picture)
- Take a bit of water and dab it onto the loose end and stick it to the roll so that it stays in a coil and doesn't unwind.
- With a rolling pin, roll out so that the coil becomes flat. Some of the onion filling will fall out and there will be a few holes in the dough. This is okay and will only make your pancake all the more yummy (see picture).
- Roll out until the pancake is about 4 - 6 inches in diameter and about 1/2 inch thick.
- Do this with the remaining 3 pieces of dough and set aside.
- Place 1 teaspoon of Earth Balance (5g) into a large nonstick skillet on low heat.
- When the Earth Balance is hot, place the pancakes in the pan and cook for 5-8 minutes, until the bottom is nice and brown.
- Add 1 more teaspoon of Earth Balance (5g) to the pan (you will have to lift up the pancakes and get it underneath each one as best you can) and flip the pancakes.
- Cook for an additional 5 - 8 minutes until the underside is brown.

cook's notes

· Other dipping sauce ideas: tahini, hummus, peanut sauce (page 133), cheese sauce (page 192) or Southern Indian Potato Curry (page 66).

Cheesy Nachos

DIFFICULTY 2½/5 LEVEL

Time: 15 - 30 minutes (plus an additional 15 - 30 minutes for the cheese sauce)
Additional recipe required
Cheese sauce, page 192
Serves 6-8

GF Gluten free
NF Soy free if making soy free cheese sauce
SF Nut free

138

1/2 of a 16 oz. bag of corn chips
1 16 oz. can refried beans (455g)
1/2 cup black olives, pitted and
sliced (65g)
½ cup green chili, canned, jar or
frozen (120g)
1 large tomato, diced (145g)
1 cup cheese sauce (page 192)
(250g)
1 avocado cut into squares
2 green onions, diced

directions

- Preheat the oven to 350°F (175°C).
- In a shallow baking dish or an oven proof skillet, place the corn chips followed by the beans, olives, green chili, tomato and cheese sauce.
- Place dish into the oven and bake for 15 minutes.
- Take out of the oven and top with avocado and green onions.

· You can use the green chili sauce on page 198 in place of the canned or jarred chilis.

cook's notes

Cornbread

DIFFICULTY
2½/5
LEVEL

Time: 30 plus minutes
Serves 6-9

NF Nut free
SF Soy free if using soy free Earth Balance buttery spread

A Little Extra Love on the Side (salads, sides and dips)

stuff you need...

1 cup cornmeal (145g)
1/2 cup polenta (85g)
1 cup whole wheat pastry flour (135g)
1/4 cup sugar (50g)
1 tablespoon baking powder (12g)
1 teaspoon sea salt (6g)
1/2 cup Earth Balance buttery spread, melted (80g)
1 cup light coconut milk (250ml)
1 tablespoon apple cider vinegar (15ml)
1 Tablespoon chia seeds (12g)

directions

- Preheat oven to 400°F (205°C).
- Lightly grease a 9x9 inch baking dish.
- In a large mixing bowl, combine the cornmeal, polenta, whole wheat pastry flour, sugar, baking soda, and salt.
- Gently combine and set aside.
- In a smaller mixing bowl, combine the coconut milk, Earth Balance, apple cider vinegar and chia seeds. Whisk to combine.
- Pour wet mixture into dry mixture and stir until just combined.
- Pour the batter into the pan and bake for 25 minutes.

cook's notes

· Do not overstir. Over stirring can cause dense cornbread.

Time: 30 plus minutes (take note that this will cook in the slow cooker for 5 hours)
Serves 6-8

GF Gluten free
NF Nut free
SF Soy free

DIFFICULTY
1½/5
LEVEL

Slow Cooker Spanish Rice

 stuff you need...

2 cups brown rice (385g)
1 onion, diced (120g)
4 garlic cloves, minced
1 green bell pepper, diced (120g)
1 carrot, diced (130g)
2 tomatoes, diced (215g)
1 can green chilies (4oz)
1 teaspoon garlic powder (4g)
2 teaspoons oregano (2g)
1/2 teaspoon turmeric
1/2 teaspoon cumin
2 tablespoons chili powder (20g)
1 teaspoon salt (6g)
2 cups vegetable broth (470ml)
2 teaspoons olive oil (10ml)

directions

- Place all of the ingredients into a large bowl and stir to combine.
- Place into a slow cooker and cook on low for 5 hours.

cook's notes

- Make sure that your broth is gluten and soy free if following those guidelines.
- If your broth is low sodium, you may need to add more salt to taste when the rice is done cooking.

Time: 5 - 15 minutes
Makes 3 1/2 cups / 595g

GF Gluten free
NF Nut free
SF Soy free

DIFFICULTY
1½
/5
LEVEL

A Little Extra Love on the Side (salads, sides and dips)

Salsa

stuff you need...

3 medium-sized tomatoes, chopped (500g)
1/2 cup red onion, diced (60g)
1 jalapeno, diced (20g)
1/4 cup cilantro leaves, lightly packed (10g)
Juice from 1 lime
3/4 teaspoon sea salt (5g)
1/4 teaspoon sugar (2g)

directions

- Place all ingredients into a mixing bowl and mix until ingredients are combined.

cook's notes

· Leave seeds in the jalapeno if you like it spicy.

Food for the Body & Soul

I Need Food Now
(super fast snacks)

Grilled Cheese Sandwich with Apple, Parsley and Pecans

Time: 5 - 15 minutes
Serves 1 (you may want to make 2 while you're at it because it's hard to eat just one of these!)

GF Gluten free if using gluten free bread
SF Soy free if using soy free Earth Balance buttery spread and soy free bread

DIFFICULTY
1/5
LEVEL

stuff you need...

2 slices sprouted wheat bread
1/4 cup jalapeno havarti wedge Daiya cheese (35g)
1 tablespoon parsley, chopped (4g)
1 tablespoon pecans, chopped (15g)
5 apple slices, cut into 1/8 inch slices (the crunchier the apple the better)
2 tablespoons Earth Balance buttery spread (30g)

directions

- Spread half of the cheese on one piece of bread and the other half on the other piece of bread.
- Heat the Earth Balance in a pan on medium - low heat.
- Place the walnuts, parsley and apples on one side of bread and cover it with the other piece of bread.
- Place sandwich in the pan and cook for 3 minutes with a lid over the pan.
- Flip over and cook for an additional 3 minutes with the pan covered.

Garden Veggie Sandwich

Time: 5 - 15 minutes
Serves 1

GF Gluten free if using gluten free bread
NF Nut free

DIFFICULTY
1/5
LEVEL

stuff you need...

2 slices sprouted wheat bread
2 tablespoons vegenaise (35g)
1 tablespoon nutritional yeast (4g)
4 or 5 sprays of Braggs Liquid Aminos
1/2 an avocado, cut into 1/2 - 1/4 inch long pieces
5 cucumber rounds
5-7 red onion rings, thinly sliced
1 romaine leaf, thinly sliced

directions

- Spread 1 tablespoon of vegenaise evenly on each slice of bread.
- Sprinkle the nutritional yeast on one slice of bread and spray the Braggs on the other slice.
- Place the avocado in a single layer on top of the nutritional yeast.
- Place the cucumber rounds on top of the Braggs.
- Place the red onion slices on top of the cucumbers.
- Place the romaine over the red onions.
- Put the two slices together and slice diagonally.

cook's notes

· This is a very basic recipe, even inexperienced cooks will be able to whip it together.
· If you like more or less of any of the ingredients then feel free to adapt it to your taste.
· If you don't have Braggs in a spray bottle then you can evenly distribute 1/4 teaspoon.

Sesame soy noodles with kale

Time: 5 - 15 minutes
Serves 4

NF **Nut free**

DIFFICULTY
2/5
LEVEL

I Need Food Now! (super fast snacks)

stuff you need...

1/2 box angel hair pasta (1/2 lb / 227g)
1 bunch of curly kale, de-stemmed and torn into bite-sized pieces (120g)
1 teaspoon sesame oil (5ml)
1/4 cup green onions, chopped (20g)

Sauce

3 tablespoons soy sauce (45ml)
2 teaspoons sesame oil (10ml)
1 teaspoon molasses (5ml)
2 teaspoons dark soy sauce (10ml)
1 teaspoon sugar (4g)
2 tablespoons water (30ml)
1 teaspoon white pepper (4g)

directions

- Cook the pasta per the directions on the box.
- While the pasta is cooking, make the sauce by adding all of the sauce ingredients into a small bowl and whisking to combine. Set aside.
- Place 6 cups of water in a pan, along with 1 teaspoon of sesame oil (5ml).
- When water reaches a boil, place the kale in the pan and cook for 1 minute and then drain the kale and set aside.
- When the pasta is done cooking, strain it and place it back in the pan.
- Pour sauce over noodles and mix well.
- Add a large scoop of pasta in the middle of each plate.
- Sprinkle with green onions.
- Place a portion of kale on the side of the pasta.

cook's notes

· If you do not have dark soy sauce on hand you can leave this out. Dark soy sauce is thicker and sweeter than regular soy sauce. It is found in Asian grocery stores.
· If you or anyone you are cooking for are meat eaters, you can easily add Beefless Tips by Gardein to this dish and the meat will not be missed.

For this you will need:
1/2 package frozen Beefless Tips
1/2 tablespoon balsamic vinegar (7.5ml)

· Heat a nonstick skillet over medium heat.
· Place the frozen Beefless Tips in the skillet and pour the balsamic vinegar over them.
· Cook on medium for 10 minutes, stirring occasionally.
· Add a portion of the Beefless Beef Tips to the pasta and continue with green onions and kale.

Sesame Blanched Kale

DIFFICULTY **1/5** **LEVEL**

Time: 5-15 minutes
Serves 1

GF Gluten free if using gluten free soy sauce
SF Soy free if using salt in place of the soy sauce
NF Nut fee

stuff you need...

3 cups water (705ml)
1/2 teaspoon sesame oil (2.5ml)
1/2 bunch kale, any variety will do (4 cups / 125g)
1/4 teaspoon Braggs Liquid Aminos or soy sauce (1ml)

directions

- Place the water and the sesame oil in a pan and bring to a boil.
- While the water is coming to a boil, wash and cut your kale. Use the leaves and the stems (cut the leaves 1-2 inches long and the stems 1/2 - 1/4 inches long).
- When water comes to a boil, turn off the heat, add the kale, stir with a spoon and let it sit for 1 minute.
- After 1 minute, drain the kale in a colander and shake off excess water.
- Place in a bowl, add the Braggs or soy sauce (or salt to taste if using that option) and stir to coat.

Quesadilla with Cashew Cheese, Tomato and Kale

Time: 5-15 minutes (does not include the cashew cheese recipe)
Additional recipe required
Cashew cheese, page 184
Serves 1

DIFFICULTY 2/5 LEVEL

SF Soy free if using soy free Earth Balance buttery spread

I Need Food Now! (super fast snacks)

2 whole wheat tortillas
4 tablespoons cashew cheese (page 184) (80g)
1/2 tomato, sliced into thin rounds
3/4 cup kale, finely sliced (20g)
1/8 teaspoon white pepper
1 tablespoon Earth Balance buttery spread (15g)

directions

- Place 2 tablespoons of cashew cheese on each tortilla and spread out evenly.
- Place the tomatoes on one of the tortillas so that none of the tomatoes are over-lapping.
- Put the kale on top of the tomatoes. Spread it out so that the kale is evenly distributed on the tortilla.
- Sprinkle the white pepper on the tortilla that has only the cashew cheese.
- Place that tortilla on top of the tortilla with the tomatoes and kale.
- Melt the Earth Balance in a large skillet.
- Place the quesadilla flat in the pan and place a lid over the pan.
- Cook for 3 minutes on medium heat.
- Flip over, cover the pan and cook for 3 more minutes.

Bagel with Cream Cheese and fresh basil

Time: 5-15 minutes
Serves 1

 **NF** Nut free

DIFFICULTY 1/5 LEVEL

1 sprouted wheat bagel
2 tablespoons vegan cream cheese
(45g)
8 cucumber rounds, thinly sliced
6 thin red onions rounds
2 large tomato rounds, sliced 1/4 inch
thick
Pinch of sea salt
1-2 large fresh basil leaves, thinly
chopped

directions

- Toast bagel and spread 1 tablespoon of vegan cream cheese on both sides.
- Place the cucumber on one half and the onions on the other half.
  Place the tomatoes on top of the cucumbers, followed by a
- pinch of salt.
- Place the basil on top of the tomatoes.
- Put both halves together and serve.

cook's notes

· I recommend vegan cream cheese by Follow Your Heart, it is creamy and delicious.

Wrap with Toasted Cumin Cashew Hummus and Dandelion Greens

Time: 5 - 15 minutes (not including the cashew hummus)
Additional recipe required:
Toasted cumin and lime cashew dip, page 116
Serves 1

DIFFICULTY
1/5
LEVEL

stuff you need...

2 teaspoons Earth Balance buttery spread (5g)
4 strips tempeh bacon
1 whole wheat tortilla
2 tablespoons toasted cumin and lime cashew dip (40g)
1/2 cup dandelion greens (8g)

directions

- Heat Earth Balance in a large skillet over medium heat.
- Add tempeh bacon and cook for two minutes on either side.
- Heat the tortilla over the burner until is is warmed on both sides (if you have an electric stove, heat a skillet and warm the tortilla in the skillet).
- Spread cashew dip evenly over the tortilla.
- Add the bacon and the dandelion greens in the center of the tortilla and wrap like a burrito.

cook's notes

· You can swap the tempeh bacon with baked tofu (page 190) for a yummy alternative filling.

Finn's BLT

DIFFICULTY
1/5
LEVEL

Time: 5 - 15 minutes
Serves 1

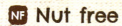 Nut free

stuff you need...

2 teaspoons Earth Balance buttery spread (5g)
4 strips tempeh bacon cut in half
1/2 teaspoon dried basil
2 slices sprouted bread
Vegan mayo
4 tomato slices
1 large romaine leaf

directions

- Heat Earth Balance evenly in a large skillet over medium heat.
- Add tempeh bacon to one side of the skillet and two slices of bread to the other side.
- Sprinkle dried basil over the tempeh bacon and cook the bacon and the bread for two minutes on either side.
- Spread Vegenaise (to your liking) on either side of the bread and add tomatoes, bacon and romaine.
- Top with second piece of bread, cut diagonally in half.

cook's notes

· We use vegan mayo by Vegenaise.

The addition of dried basil was my 12 year old nephew, Finn's, culinary twist.

· He loves to make this sandwich and I love to eat it. The dried basil gives it an unexpected depth of flavor. Thank you Finn!

Creamy Cucumber Dulse Salad

DIFFICULTY
1/5
LEVEL

Time: 5 - 15 minutes
Serves 2

GF Gluten free
SF Soy free if using soy free Vegenaise
NF Nut free

stuff you need...

1 cucumber, peeled, cut into 1/4 inch rounds and then cut in half

1/4 cup red onion, thinly sliced

Sauce
1/4 cup Vegenaise (50g)
1 teaspoon dulse flakes (2g)
1/2 teaspoon sugar (4g)
1/2 teaspoon apple cider vinegar (2.5ml)

directions

- Place cucumbers and onions in a medium-sized bowl.
- In a small bowl, place all of the sauce ingredients and whisk to combine.
- Pour dressing over cucumbers and onions and stir to coat.

cook's notes

· This side dish goes nicely with veggie fried rice (page 128). See description of dulse on page 9 if you are unfamiliar.

Carrot Raisin Salad with Fennel and Walnuts

Time: 5 - 15 minutes
Serves 4

GF Gluten free
SF Soy free if using soy free vegan mayo

I Need Food Now! (super fast snacks)

stuff you need...

3 carrots, peeled and grated (3 cups / 285g)
1/2 cup raisins (60g)
1 fennel bulb, sliced into thin slices (50g)
1/2 cup walnuts, chopped (45g)
1/4 cup fresh parsley, chopped (4g)
1/4 cup vegan mayo (60g)
1/2 teaspoon apple cider vinegar (2.5ml)
1 teaspoon lemon juice (5ml)

directions

- Place all ingredients into a large bowl and mix until everything is combined.

cook's notes

· I use vegan mayo by Vegenaise.

Almond Butter and Fruit Sandwich

DIFFICULTY **1/5** LEVEL

Time: 5 - 15 minutes
Serves 1

SF **Soy free if using soy free Earth Balance and soy free bread**

2 slices of sprouted grain bread
Earth Balance buttery spread
Almond butter
Fruit (blueberries, pear slices, apple slices, strawberries are all yummy suggestions)
Chopped nuts (almonds, walnuts and pecans are all yummy suggestions)

directions

- Toast the bread.
- Spread Earth Balance on either side followed by the almond butter.
- Place fruit on top of almond butter and sprinkle with chopped nuts.
- Serve open face.

Cheesy Spinach Dip

DIFFICULTY 2/5 LEVEL

Time: 5 - 15 minutes
Serves 2 - 4 as a snack/appetizer

GF Gluten free
NF Nut free
SF Soy free if using soy free vegan mayo and soy free Earth Balance buttery spread

stuff you need...

1 tablespoon Earth Balance buttery spread (15g)
1/2 yellow onion, chopped (100g)
1 bunch fresh spinach, chopped (6 cups/315g)
1/2 cup vegan mayo (100g)
1/4 teaspoon salt

cook's notes

· Be sure to use fresh spinach

directions

- In a large skillet heat Earth Balance and cook onions for 3 minutes.
- Add spinach and cook for an additional 2 minutes.
- Place onion/spinach mixture in a colander and drain as much of the liquid as you can by pressing into the sides of the strainer.
- Place mixture in the food processor and pulse several times just until everything is chopped.
- Place spinach in bowl and add the mayo and salt and stir.

Bruschetta with Toast Points

DIFFICULTY **2/5** LEVEL

Time: 5 - 15 minutes
Serves 4 (as an appetizer)

GF Gluten free if using gluten free bread
NF Nut free
SF Soy free

I Need Food Now! (super fast snacks)

3 medium-sized tomatoes, diced (420g)
4 garlic cloves, minced
1 bunch of fresh basil, thinly chopped (35g)
1/2 teaspoon salt (3g)
2 teaspoons balsamic vinegar (10ml)
1 tablespoon olive oil (15ml)
1 teaspoon lemon juice (5ml)
6 pieces of bread, toasted and cut into fourths

directions

- In medium-sized mixing bowl, add all of the ingredients except the bread and stir to combine.
- Toast and cut the bread.
- Place the toasted bread on a large plate and place 2 heaping spoons of bruschetta on each piece of toast.

Pineapple Salsa in Pineapple Bowl

DIFFICULTY **3/5** LEVEL

Time: 5 - 15 minutes
Serves 6-8

GF Gluten free
NF Nut free
SF Soy free

stuff you need...

3 cups pineapple, diced into 1/2 inch pieces (485g)

3 medium tomatoes, diced (425g)

3 garlic cloves, minced

1/4 cup jalapenos, minced (30g)

1/4 cup red onions, diced (30g)

1/2 cup cilantro leaves (8g)

1/2 teaspoon salt (3g)

Juice from half a lime

directions Pineapple Bowl

- Cut the pineapple in half.
- Take the bottom half and cut around the circumference of the pineapple as close to the edge as possible. Don't cut too deep because you don't want to puncture the bottom of the pineapple.
- Cut a line through the circular section (again, not going too deep).
- And then cut that in fourths. You will now have four sections that need taken out.
- Use a large spoon to scoop out all 4 sections. You don't have to be too careful about getting out the chunks neatly, it is more important that you don't puncture the bottom of the pineapple.
- You now have your pineapple bowl ready to go.

Salsa

- Mix all of the ingredients together in a large mixing bowl.
- Scoop salsa into the pineapple bowl and serve with corn chips.

cook's notes

· You don't have to make the bowl if you are in a hurry. It is purely for presentation.

Food for the Body & Soul

Eggless Egg Salad

DIFFICULTY 2/5 LEVEL

Time: 15 - 30 minutes
Serves 6

GF Gluten free
NF Nut free

stuff you need...

 directions

Salad
3 cups extra firm tofu (415g)
3 celery stalks, diced (2 cups/ 250g)
1/2 yellow onion, diced (1 cup/ 122g)
1/4 cup parsley, chopped (15g)

Sauce
1 cup vegan mayo (230g)
1 teaspoon apple cider vinegar (5ml)
1/2 cup nutritional yeast (30g)
1/2 teaspoon dill
1/4 teaspoon turmeric
1/4 teaspoon white pepper
1 teaspoon dulse flakes (2g)
1 teaspoon sugar (6g)
1/2 teaspoon salt (3g)
3 turns fresh black pepper

- Drain and rinse tofu with water and dab with a clean kitchen cloth to absorb some of the moisture.
- Place the celery, onion and parsley in a large bowl.
- Crumble the tofu into the bowl with the celery, onions and parsley.
- Crumbling the tofu with your hands is the most effective method. Crumble until there are no more big chunks.
- In a separate smaller bowl, add all of the sauce ingredients and whisk to combine.
- Add the sauce to the tofu/veggie mixture and stir until thoroughly combined.

- Serve with crackers, on toasted bread, in romaine leaves or endive.
- Garnishing with raisins or dried cranberries is highly encouraged.
- Find out all about Dulse on page 9.
- We use vegan mayo by vegenaise.

 cook's notes

Curry Roasted Cauliflower

DIFFICULTY
2/5
LEVEL

Time: 15 - 30 minutes
Serves 4 - 6 as a snack or side

GF Gluten free
NF Nut free
SF Soy free

I Need Food Now! (super fast snacks)

1 large head of cauliflower, leaves trimmed and cut into bite-sized pieces

1 red onion (175g), sliced into thin rings and then cut in half (or cut into half and then cut into thin half rings)

2 tablespoons olive oil plus 1 teaspoon, divided

2 teaspoons whole cumin seeds

2 teaspoons curry powder

1 teaspoon garam masala

5 turns fresh black pepper

1 teaspoon salt (6g)

3 teaspoons lime juice, divided

directions

- Preheat oven to 425°F (220°C).
- In a large mixing bowl, place cauliflower and onions and set aside.
- Heat 1 teaspoon of olive oil in a small skillet.
- Add cumin seeds and cook for 30 seconds to 1 minute on low heat, stirring occasionally as not to burn.
- Turn off heat and place seeds over cauliflower and onions along with 2 teaspoons of the lime juice.
- In a separate small mixing bowl add curry powder, garam masala, black pepper and salt; stir to combine.
- Pour spice mixture over the cauliflower and onions along with 2 tablespoons of olive oil.
- Mix well to combine all ingredients.
- Place on a parchment paper covered baking sheet and bake for 25 minutes.
- Take out of oven and squeeze 1 teaspoon of lime juice over the cauliflower.
- Serve warm or at room temperature.

· This recipe is way better if you use red onions.

· If you are using a really big head of cauliflower then you may need to add a little more olive oil.

cook's notes

Cold Tofu Poke

DIFFICULTY
2/5
LEVEL

Time: 5 - 15 minutes
Serves 2 - 4 as a snack or side

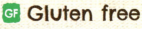 Gluten free
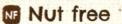 Nut free

I Need Food Now! (super fast snacks)

stuff you need...

1 package (14 oz. / 397g) firm tofu cut in 1/2 inch cubes
2 tablespoons dried Wakame seaweed (6g) soaked in 2 cups of water (475ml) for at least 10 minutes.
3 tablespoons soy sauce (45ml)
2 teaspoons sesame oil (10ml)
2 teaspoons lime juice (10ml)
2 cloves garlic, minced
1/2 cup red onion, finely diced (50g)
1 teaspoon, peeled and grated ginger (4g)
2 green onions, sliced (1/2 cup / 30g)

directions

- Soak the seaweed and set aside.
- Cut the tofu, place in a bowl and put in the refrigerator while you prepare the rest of the ingredients.
- Place the soy sauce, sesame oil, lime juice, garlic, red onion, ginger and green onions in a small bowl and mix to combine.
- Drain the seaweed and chop until it is in small pieces. Place seaweed into the bowl along with the rest of the sauce and veggies.
- Take the tofu out of the fridge and pour sauce/seaweed mixture over it.
- With your hands, gently stir the tofu.
- Serve cold.

cook's notes

· With some types of seaweed (i.e Arame) you will not need to cut pieces; it will be small enough as is.
· You can use tap or cold water to soak the seaweed.
· Add soy sauce to taste if needed

Food for the Body & Soul

Etcetera, etcetera, etcetera...
(sub recipes and miscellaneous)

Cashew Cheese

DIFFICULTY 2/5 LEVEL

Time: 30 plus minutes (this is because the cashews need to soak. Once the cashews are soaked it will take about 10 minutes).
Makes 1 cup / 210g

GF Gluten free
SF Soy free

Etcetera, etcetera, etcetera...(sub recipes and miscellaneous)

stuff you need... · 1 cup cashews (130g) soaked in 3 cups (709 ml) of water for at least 1 hour.
2 teaspoons lemon juice (10ml)
1/2 teaspoon salt (3g)
2 turns fresh black pepper
1/4 cup water (60ml)

 directions

- Soak, drain and rinse cashews.
- Place in a food processor, along with lemon juice, salt and black pepper.
- Pulse for about 1 minute to combine ingredients.
- Add water and process until completely smooth, about 2 -4 minutes.

 cook's notes

· You can soak the cashews up to overnight. The longer you soak them the creamier the final product will be.
· You may want to turn off the food processor and scrape down the cheese from the sides a couple of times.
· Think of this as a base recipe. From here, you can add chives, garlic, rosemary, whatever you want to make it fancy.

Basic Red Sauce

DIFFICULTY 2/5 LEVEL

Time: 15 - 30 minutes
Makes 4 1/2 cups / 1.2kg

GF Gluten free
NF Nut free
SF Soy free

Etcetera, etcetera, etcetera...(sub recipes and miscellaneous)

stuff you need...

3 tablespoons olive oil

1 yellow onion, diced (245g)

6 garlic cloves, minced

3 cups mushrooms, sliced (200g)

7 roma tomatoes, diced (450g)

2 tablespoons tomato paste (40g)

1 can tomato sauce (15oz / 426g)

1 bunch fresh basil leaves, chopped (30g)

1/2 tablespoon dried oregano (2g)

1/2 tablespoon dried basil (2g)

1 teaspoon sea salt (6g)

directions 1 tablespoon sugar (15g)

- Heat olive oil in a large pot and saute the onions and garlic for 3 minutes.
- Add the mushrooms and cook for 3 additional minutes.
- Add tomatoes, tomato paste, tomato sauce, fresh basil, dried oregano, dried basil, salt and sugar.
  simmer on low for 20 minutes.

cook's notes · If you make the sauce a day in advance, the flavors will be more pronounced and delicious.

Jalapeño Lime Slaw

Time: 5-15 minutes
Makes 4 cups / 355g

GF Gluten free
NF Nut free
SF Soy free

Etcetera, etcetera, etcetera...(sub recipes and miscellaneous)

stuff you need...

1/4 head red cabbage, thinly sliced (3 cups / 170g)

1/4 head green cabbage, thinly sliced (3 cups / 170g)

1 large jalapeno, seeds taken out and then sliced (35g)

Juice from 1 lime

Juice from 1/2 teaspoon peeled and grated ginger (squeeze juice from ginger with your fingers)

1/4 teaspoon salt (1.5g)

1 teaspoon sugar (6g)

directions

- Place all ingredients into a large bowl and toss to combine.

Sesame Ginger Baked Tofu

Time: 30 plus minutes (you will need to marinate the tofu over night. After you marinate the tofu it will take 15 minutes) Makes 1 1/4 cups / 165g

GF Gluten free
NF Nut free

1 box firm tofu (12 oz./340g), marinated overnight.

Marinade

1/4 cup soy sauce (60ml)

2 tablespoons rice vinegar (30ml)

2 tablespoons mirin (30ml)

2 teaspoons sesame oil (10ml)

3 cloves garlic, grated

1 teaspoon ginger, peeled and grated (6g)

2 tablespoons olive oil (30ml)

1/2 teaspoon 5-spice powder (2g)

2 tablespoons water (30ml)

directions

- Drain and rinse tofu and pat to dry with a clean kitchen cloth.
- Place on a cutting board and slice into 1/4 to 1/2 inch-thick pieces.
- Place in a shallow container that has a lid.
- Make the marinade by placing all of the marinade ingredients into a small bowl and whisking to combine.
- Pour marinade over the tofu, making sure that marinade is covering each piece of tofu as much as possible.
- Cover with a lid and refrigerate overnight.
- Preheat oven to 375°F (190°C).
- Bake for 15 minutes, turn over and bake for an additional 15 minutes.

Cheese Sauce

Time: 15 - 30 minutes
Makes 3 cups / 700g

DIFFICULTY
2/5
LEVEL

GF Gluten free
NF Nut free
SF Soy free if using soy free Earth
Balance buttery spread

stuff you need...

1 russet potato, peeled and cut into bite-sized pieces (1 1/2 cups / 240g)

1 cup carrot, cut into 1/2 inch rounds (130g)

1/4 yellow onion, diced (1/2 cup / 65g)

2 cups water (475 ml)

1/2 cup Earth Balance buttery spread (70g)

1/2 cup nutritional yeast (40g)

1/2 teaspoon turmeric

1 teaspoon salt (6g)

3 tablespoons coconut milk (45 ml)

3 turns fresh black pepper

directions

- Place potato, carrot and onion in a pan with 2 cups of water and simmer for 20 minutes with the lid on.
- After 20 minutes, turn off heat and add Earth Balance, nutritional yeast, turmeric and salt. Stir to combine until melted.
- Pour mixture into a blender and blend until creamy, about one minute on medium. You may need to scrape the sides down from the blender a couple of times for everything to get incorporated.
- Add coconut milk to the blender and continue to blend until mixture is creamy throughout.
- Place into a bowl and add fresh black pepper.

Stovetop Cilantro Brown rice

Time: 30 plus minutes
Makes 3 cups (410g)

GF Gluten free
NF Nut free
SF Soy free

Etcetera, etcetera, etcetera...(sub recipes and miscellaneous)

1 cup brown rice (180g)
2 cups water
1/2 cup cilantro stems and leaves,
chopped (20g)
1 tablespoon olive oil (15ml)
1/4 teaspoon sea salt (2g)

directions

- Rinse and strain rice.
- In a medium-sized pan, place water, cilantro, olive oil and sea salt and rinsed rice.
- Bring to a low boil.
- Stir, place a lid on the pan, turn the heat to very low and cook for 30-40 minutes until water is absorbed and rice is fully cooked.

· The higher the elevation the longer it will take to cook.
· Check after 25 minutes to see how close it is to being done.

cook's
notes

Pie Crust 2 ways

Time: 30 plus minutes
Choose from Traditional or Gluten Free

Etcetera, etcetera, etcetera...(sub recipes and miscellaneous)

Traditional Crust

Makes 2 pie crusts

 SF Soy free is using soy free Earth Balance buttery spread

NF Nut free

Gluten Free Crust

Makes 2 pie crusts

SF Soy free is using soy free Earth Balance buttery spread

NF Nut free

GF Gluten free

stuff you need...

1 1/2 cups whole wheat pastry flour (400g)
1/2 teaspoon salt (3g)
1 cup Earth Balance buttery spread (120g)
3/4 cup ice water (175ml)

stuff you need...

2 cups rice flour (300g)
1/2 cup garbanzo flour (80g)
1/2 teaspoon salt (3g)
1 cup Earth Balance buttery spread (120g)
3/4 cup ice water (175ml)

directions

- Place the flour, Earth Balance and a glass mixing bowl in the freezer and chill for 10 - 15 minutes.
- Place 2 cups of water in a bowl and fill it with ice cubes. Set aside.
- When items in freezer are done chilling, put the flour and salt in the chilled bowl and whisk to combine.
- Cut in Earth Balance with a pastry cutter, a fork or two knives.
- Add in ice water one tablespoon at a time, gently mixing after each tablespoon is added.
- The consistency of the dough should be in between crumbly and wet. You want it wet enough just to hold together.
- When the correct consistency is reached, take the dough and roll it into a ball.
- Place the dough ball in a plastic bag and gently press (through the plastic) into a flat disc about 1 inch high, making sure that no air gets into the bag.
- Place in the refrigerator for 30 minutes.
- Proceed with whatever recipe calls for a crust.

· If the dough is not coming together and still crumbly, add 1 more tablespoon of water.
· The gluten free pie crust may be a little harder to handle since it lacks the gluten. If you have to patch it together a little that is is fine, it will still taste yummy.

cook's notes

Green Chili Sauce

Time: 15 - 30 minutes
Makes 4 cups / 1kg

DIFFICULTY 2/5 LEVEL

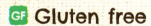

GF Gluten free
NF Nut free
SF Soy free

Etcetera, etcetera, etcetera...(sub recipes and miscellaneous)

stuff you need...

2 tablespoons canola oil (30ml)

1 yellow onion, diced (220g)

4 garlic cloves, minced

3 cups mushrooms, finely chopped (190g)

2 cups green chili, peeled and diced (400g)

1 tablespoon onion granules (10g)

1 tablespoon garlic granules (12g)

1 teaspoon salt (6g)

1/4 cup rice flour (45g)

2 cups vegetable broth (470ml)

directions

- Heat oil in a large skillet on medium heat.
- Add onions and garlic and saute for 5 minutes, stirring occasionally.
- Add mushrooms and cook for for 2 minutes.
- Add green chili, onion granules, garlic granules and salt, stir and cook for 1 minute.
- Add flour and stir well for 1 minute. Sauce should be getting thick at this point.
- Slowly pour in the broth, stirring constantly. Once all the broth is poured in, turn heat to low and stir for for 3 minutes, allowing the sauce to thicken.

cook's notes

· You can use fresh, frozen, canned or jarred green chili. The fresher the chilies the more tasty the sauce.

Spiced Roasted Potatoes

Time: 30 plus minutes
Makes 6 cups / 780g

DIFFICULTY
2½/5
LEVEL

GF Gluten free
NF Nut free
SF Soy free

Etcetera, etcetera, etcetera...(sub recipes and miscellaneous)

stuff you need...

4 medium red potatoes, cut into bite-sized pieces (6 cups / 815g)
3 tablespoons olive oil (45ml)
1/2 teaspoon cumin (2g)
1 teaspoon chili powder (4g)
1 teaspoon oregano
2 teaspoons garlic powder (8g)
1/2 teaspoon sea salt (3g)

directions

- Preheat oven to 350°F (175°C).
- Place the cut potatoes into a large mixing bowl.
- Add the olive oil, cumin, chili powder, oregano, garlic powder, and sea salt.
- Mix to combine ingredients.
- Place on a baking sheet in a single layer and bake for 30 minutes.
- Turn heat up to 400°F (205°C) and bake for an additional 10 minutes.

Anasazi Beans

DIFFICULTY
2/5
LEVEL

Time: 30 plus minutes
(Keep in mind that you will have to soak the beans overnight)

Makes 4 1/4 cups (870g)

GF Gluten free
NF Nut free
SF Soy free

Etcetera, etcetera, etcetera...(sub recipes and miscellaneous)

stuff you need...

2 cups dry Anasazi Beans (355g),
soaked in 5 cups of water overnight
1 tablespoon olive oil (15ml)
1 teaspoon salt (6g)
1 tablespoon onion powder (10g)

directions

- Drain and rinse the beans (Sort through to make sure there are no pebbles or funky beans) and place them in the pressure cooker.
- Add 6 cups of water and the olive oil.
- Place the lid on the pressure cooker and lock it.
- Place the valve on the lid and turn the heat to high.
- Allow the pot to come to pressure.
- Cook for 25 minutes after the pressure cooker starts hissing.
- After 25 minutes, turn off heat and allow to cool, about 10-15 minutes. If you are in a hurry, carefully bring the pot to the sink and run cold water over the lid until the pressure has gone down.

Garbanzo Beans

Time: 30 plus minutes
(Keep in mind that you will have to soak
the beans overnight)

Makes 2 1/2 cups / 410g

GF **Gluten free**
NF **Nut free**
SF **Soy free**

DIFFICULTY
2/5
LEVEL

Etcetera, etcetera, etcetera...(sub recipes and miscellaneous)

stuff you need... 1 cup dry garbanzo beans (180g) soaked in 4 cups (945ml) of water overnight

1 tablespoon olive oil (15ml)

directions

- Drain and rinse the beans (sort through to make sure there are no pebbles or funky beans) and place them in the pressure cooker.
- Add 6 cups of water and the olive oil.
- Place the lid on the pressure cooker and lock it.
- Place the valve on the lid and turn the heat to high.
- Allow the pot to come to pressure.
- Cook for 25 minutes after the pressure cooker starts hissing.
- After 25 minutes, turn off heat and allow to cool, about 10-15 minutes. If you are in a hurry, carefully bring the pot to the sink and run cold water over the lid until the pressure has gone down.

Pinto Beans

Time: 30 plus minutes

Makes 4 cups / 950g
(Keep in mind that you will have to soak the beans overnight)

GF Gluten free

NF Nut free

SF Soy free

DIFFICULTY
2/5
LEVEL

Etcetera, etcetera, etcetera...(sub recipes and miscellaneous)

stuff you need...

1 1/2 cups dried beans (285g), soaked in 6 cups (1.4 liters) of water overnight
1 yellow onion, cut into eighths (215g)
5 cloves of garlic, left whole
1 teaspoon cumin (2g)
1 tablespoon red chili powder (10g)
1/2 cup cilantro, chopped. Use stems and leaves (30g)
1 tablespoon olive oil (15ml)
6 cups water (1.4 liters)
1 teaspoon salt (6g)

directions

- Drain and rinse the beans (sort through to make sure there are no pebbles or other funky items) and place them in the pressure cooker.
- Add the onion, garlic, cumin, red chili powder, cilantro, and olive oil.
- Turn heat to medium, and saute for 5 minutes, stirring frequently.
- Add the water and stir again to combine the ingredients.
- Place the lid on the pressure cooker and lock it.
- Place the valve on the lid and turn the heat to high.
- Allow the pot to come to pressure.
- Cook for 30 minutes after the pressure cooker starts hissing.
- After 30 minutes, turn off heat and allow to cool on its own, about 10-15 minutes. If you are in a hurry then carefully bring the pot to the sink and run cold water over the lid until the pressure has gone down.

Sweet and savory (and slightly spicy) festive popcorn

DIFFICULTY 2/5 LEVEL

Time: 15 - 30 minutes
Serves 4 - 6 as a snack

GF Gluten free
SF Soy free if using soy free Earth Balance buttery spread

Etcetera, etcetera, etcetera...(sub recipes and miscellaneous)

stuff you need...

1 cup pecans, coarsely chopped and toasted (100g)

8 cups of popped popcorn (60g), about 1/2 cup of popcorn kernels (105g)

1/2 cup dried cranberries (65g)

1/4 teaspoon cinnamon

1/4 teaspoon cayenne pepper

1/2 teaspoon salt (4g)

1/4 cup Earth Balance buttery spread (35g)

1/4 cup brown sugar (40g)

2 tablespoons water (30ml)

Juice from 1/2 lime

directions

- Preheat oven to 300°F (150°C).
- Place pecans in a heated dry cast iron skillet and cook on medium/low heat for 5 minutes, stirring and turning over frequently so the pecans do not burn.
- Place pecans in a large bowl, along with the popped popcorn, cranberries, cinnamon, cayenne pepper and salt. Stir to combine ingredients.
- In a small saucepan, add the Earth Balance, brown sugar, water and lime juice and heat on medium for 5 minutes, stirring frequently.
- Drizzle the butter / sugar mixture over the popcorn and stir so that all of the kernels get coated.
- Place in the oven for 10 minutes, take out and let cool for another 10 minutes before serving.

INDEX

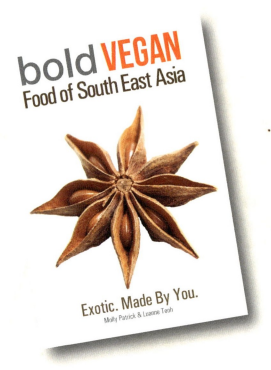

Our other publication;
Bold Vegan-Food of South East Asia.

www.boldvegan.com

end

Made in the USA
Lexington, KY
17 February 2015